POSITIVE BENEFITS

OF ASTROLOGY

Doris Chase Doane, FAFA

Published by
The American Federation of Astrologers, Inc.
P. O. Box 2240
Tempe, Arizona   85285-2040

First Printing 1992
ISBN: 0-86690-410-7
Library of Congress Catalog Card Number: 91-77114

Cover Design: Swedish artist Christel Bonnett

Published by
American Federation of Astrologers, Inc.
PO Box 22040
Tempe, AZ 85285-2040

Printed in United States of America

POSITIVE BENEFITS OF ASTROLOGY

Doris Chase Doane

Books by Doris Chase Doane

Accurate World Horoscopes
Astrologers Question Box, Volume 1
Astrologers Question Box, Volume 2
Astrology as a Business
Astrology of Childbirth
Astrology Rulerships
Astrology: 30 Years Research
Contest Charts
Doane's 1981-1985 World Wide Time Change Update
Doane's 1986-1990 World Wide Time Change Update
Horoscopes of the U.S. Presidents
How to Prepare and Pass an Astrologer's Certificate Exam
How to Read Cosmodynes
Index to the Brotherhood of Light Lessons
Positive Benefits of Astrology
Profit By Electional Astrology
Progressions in Action
Tarot Card Spread Reader (With K. Keyes)
Time Changes in Canada and Mexico
Time Changes in USA
Time Changes in the World
Vocational Selection and Counseling, Volume 1
Vocational Selection and Counseling, Volume 2
Zodiac: Key to Career (With C. Peel

CONTENTS

1 Make Your Own Happiness 1
2 Your Public Relations 5
3 Locating Horoscope Houses 9
4 Zodiacal Signs and Adaptability 14
5 A Happy Home 18
6 The Mysterious Eighth House 22
7 Find Friends in Your Horoscope 25
8 Make Your Convention Colorful 29
9 Your Jewel in the Zodiac 35
10 The Accident Syndrome 40
11 The Youthful Outlook 45
12 Differences Marked in Personality 50
13 Do Sun-Saturn Afflictions Deny Success? 54
14 Handling Mars Square Neptune 59
15 At What Degree is your Temper? 65
16 Are you Familiar with Pluto? 70
17 Make the Most of your Days 75
18 The Motherhood Principle 80
19 Demonstrating your Heart's Desire 84

BIBLIOGRAPHY

DORIS CHASE DOANE
Astrology of Childbirth. AFA. Tempe AZ. 1988.

Astrology: 30 Years Research, AFA. Tempe AZ. 1956.

How to Read Cosmodynes, AFA. Tempe AZ. 1974.

Profit by Electional Astrology, AFA. Tempe AZ. 1990.

LYNNE PALMER
Astrological Almanac. AFA. Tempe AZ. Annual.

C.C. ZAIN
Astrological Signatures. C of L. Los Angeles CA.

Mental Alchemy. C of L. Los Angeles CA. 1936.

AFA = American Federation of Astrologers, Inc.

C of L = Church of Light, Inc.

Chapter 1

MAKE YOUR OWN HAPPINESS

Happiness is at once complicated and simple. Our viewpoint, which is the result of past conditioning, will select for itself the complexity or simplicity with which happiness is associated within each of us. Modern psychiatrists agree that our attitude, the way we look at events, is the determining factor in happiness. Thus habits of all types contribute to or detract from that much sought-after state.

If we are not happy, then the key lies in correcting our attitude, or habit-systems, which relate to every department of life. The birth chart alone gives an inventory of the person's potentials, but unless we add the case history of conditioning energy, we cannot tell if the person has developed or stifled the inherent potentials or desires mapped in his horoscope.

Home environment and the idea of what a home should be is portrayed by the fourth house of the horoscope. Aside from the astrological information revealed, there are certain psychological fundamentals which need consideration. As the fourth house is a psychic house, its problems are closely related to the problems of the other houses in the psychic trinity. These are the eighth house of death, taxes and regeneration, and the twelfth house of philanthropy, hidden matters, and disappointments. How we face the problems of these departments of life has a pronounced bearing on our happiness.

Possibly one of the chief contributing causes to discord in the home is the clash of personalities which can be resolved by comparing birth charts of the persons involved in order to make suggestions to help work out the conflicts. But, in my opinion, propaganda from all avenues of expression has a place in any transmutation attempted. How a person reacts habitually to propaganda contributes to the sum total of his behavior pattern.

Two types stand out. The band-wagon type, or everybody-is-doing-it-so-you-should and the keeping up with the Jones' type, or purchasing all new items and doing all things that the Jones' do.

A universal truth should be stressed at this time: *No soul is ever free or independent as long as it allows anything or anybody to make decisions as to what actions it should take.*

Let's stop now and then to think of our reactions, to enter the silence and indulge in a bit of self-psychoanalysis. Why do we act the way we do? Are the thoughts and feelings we nourish habitually of the constructive type? Do they fit into our particular pattern of demonstrating success?

Last night the boys at the club were all talking about their successes. One has finally cleared the mortgage on his new up-and-coming business venture. Another has just been promoted to regional manager, and still another reports that his latest invention has been received with great success. As you came from the meeting, did you feel self-pity and wonder why these achievements had not come to *deserving* you?

Or maybe at work yesterday, the girl at the desk next to yours arrived all decked out in a new winter outfit, with an new, attractive hairdo that really made her looks and personality blossom. Did you compliment her sincerely, or did you envy her so much that you couldn't speak.

Your best friend drives up the latest model car. In your mind you see the 4 year old bus of yours in the garage. Do you fuss and worry about it and feel that you *must* have a new car even though yours serves the purpose for which you bought it?

If such negative reactions are habitual, chances for happiness are slim indeed. Worrying about such things is a waste of food mental energy which could be directed into a constructive channel of attaining what you want, if you know what you want. Furthermore, the mental turmoil caused by these conflicting and negative thoughts detracts from peach of mind, one of the elements of happiness.

Therefore, one step toward the happiness goal is to stop keeping up with the Jones' and to correct the want-habit of desiring so-and-so just because Tom or Dick has one. We need not envy the good fortune of our friends, for if we look closely enough, we also have many things to be thankful for. Let's resolve to develop our own talents and potentials.

In regard to our neighbors, we can use a different part of the anatomy for expressions. Instead of sticking our noses into their business, let's take a healthy interest and at the same time extend a smile and a pat on the back.

Success comes in many steps to a goal. That old adage implies that: Change is the watchword of progression. Each of us has to make adjustments to constantly changing environment. The pattern of each person's life is different than that of another.

People have only a few events in common: Birth, adolescence, maturity. At some time in life all of us face death, the transition to the inner world, and some of us have to cope with the loss of a loved one.

I have known people who have feared death for years. That fear was the outstanding factor in breeding their unhappiness. If we look at the situation intelligently, practicing faith in God, we can resolve such a fear of our own death, or resolve the bereavement and loss at the passing of our loved ones.

If we do not face the possibility openly and in advance, the loss of a loved one could become a crisis. It means the breaking up of a relationship on which we have come to depend. A religion or philosophy of life is necessary in making the adjustment.

If we understand that life is continuous and that physical death only means moving the consciousness into another environment, just as we move our home from one city to another. Being aware of the fact that the loved one will adjust to the new life more quickly if we do not detain him by mourning, we can pass this period more easily.

Perhaps at this time we make a most grievous error by trying to hide our sorrow and grief. That is regression. Would it not be better to open the emotional gates and let go, once and for all? But let's be natural about it. There is no need to prolong the emotional release. All people have a different temperament, thus release comes in different ways. After release, normal life starts taking place again. It is at this point that a good sound philosophy is needed. Let's get it beforehand.

Another great cause of unhappiness is "aging". However, this can be one of the most beautiful and fruitful periods in life if we plan for it. We might as well do so, because it is an inevitable adjustment to be faced by everyone.

As in the case of other adjustments, this change demands a rearrangement of goals. Because of the fact that physical strength and energy wanes, we must set aside some of the enthusiastic, youthful ambitions we once held. This turning-point in life can be taken gracefully. Even so, it is not necessary to retreat into age before one's time. Those who adjust easily do so because they have nourished resources to sustain them at this time. Those resources should be built into the consciousness ahead of time. It all depends upon early preparation for aging.

Perhaps the most encouraging fact is that even though physical strength diminishes with age, the imagination and creativity are effected hardly at all and can be used not only in developing skills and interests but in shaping emotional reactions and attitudes.

A shining example was when Grandma Moses took up painting when she was in her nineties. Hers was an excellent example of the creative inner resources expressing in old age.

Adjustment will be easier if we live today, plan for the future (no need to live in the past--life is ahead). If we avoid boredom like the mischief by seeking new and ever new interests, and above all, if we act and dress our own age, associating with people of the same *mental* age, we will be building habits that determine happiness.

The predisposition toward certain habit-systems is mapped in the horoscope. Reactions, pleasurable or painful, to the environment equal a person's conditioning energy.

We can gradually learn to control and direct reaction, thus achieving a set of habit-systems that are harmonious. The road map to follow is pointed out in the birth chart of each person. When that road is followed successfully, happiness is ours.

4

Chapter 2

YOUR PUBLIC RELATIONS

Public relations! What has that got to do with me? It has a lot to do with the patterns you weave into your life. These patterns are the forerunners of happiness or sadness. You can have happiness or not, depending upon how well you keep your public relations in hand.

Did you know that no action any individual takes is ever entirely independent? In the first place, it takes considerable cooperation of many people just to insure that you stay alive. Realization of that fact alone shows that happiness depends upon getting along with other people.

In your horoscope, you will find the best index of how you will get along with others at different times in your life if you do nothing to change it. the so-called "association" horoscope houses embrace the departments of life that picture the people in your environment.

The Trinity of Association is composed of three horoscope houses -- third, seventh and eleventh. The planets in these houses, the signs and aspects involved give the clue to how to you can keep your public relations in hand.

Relatives in general, but brothers and sisters in particular, are ruled by the third house. When aspects form to stimulate this department of life, the prepared astrological student knows it before hand and takes precautionary measures. So it is with the other houses.

The seventh house rules acquaintances, other people in general (the masses), the partner and the husband or wife. The eleventh house rules

5

personal friends, impersonal acquaintances as well as counselors.

In your daily life you brush shoulders with the three classes of people mapped by the Association Trinity. As you look back over a period of time, you can remember the days when you said, "Everything went wrong!" Chances are that people figured prominently in the causes of the upset. If you had known the aspects ahead of time, you would have had a more than even chance of beating the discord which would otherwise manifest.

Say, if you are under the impact of energies mapped by a Mars - Mercury aspect which leads into the association houses, then you will have to watch your tongue. These planets in combination coincide with the sharp, abrupt and unthoughtful things which are said and can never be recalled.

Under these periods of stimulation concentrate upon being a good listener. It is an art and will take some effort to accomplish at these times. The best method is to learn to listen to a story all the way to its finish before making any comment. Keep your eyes on the speaker and give him your attention.

This situation is no place for the dead-pan expression. Interest can be aroused if we try hard enough. Relaxation while listening helps you to think more clearly and with more unity. Tangents of thoughts and flights of ideas cannot breed in the place of relaxed, directed attention.

If you will accomplish doing those things, then the sound of your own voice will not be mandatory and you will be a good listener. For excellent public relations, being a good, attentive listener comes very near the top of the list. If the approach of *listening* is taken, the impulsive, harsh comments will not be expressed. Then the energy of the Mars-Mercury aspect can be directed into a constructive channel.

This energy cannot be repressed. It will express! It will express itself in a Mars-Mercury manner of some sort. The twist to effective living is to make the decision yourself as to just how that energy will be allowed to manifest constructively.

Recently a successful salesman told about the great change that had come into his life since he had astrological assistance. In his position, he makes personal contacts with many kinds of people all day long. Before he knew about astrology and the aspects that form in a horoscope, he had his "off" days. He would be caught unawares by his first customer of the day, and there would be one complaint after another. That set the trend for the day. No matter what he did he couldn't seem to change the vibration.

Since he now looks ahead to his "adverse" days he is prepared and uses a different approach with not only his customers but how he schedules his work plan. Now he claims he seldom has a day that starts off on the wrong foot, so to speak. He has discovered how astrology can help in keeping his public relations in hand.

In thinking of our public relations we sometimes place incorrect values on things. Margaret Chase Smith, while serving in the United States Congress, was an outstanding politician to whom public relations were important. But if you examined her record, you would find that she didn't have some of the things that many people think are absolutely necessary to get places and be something.

She only had a high school education. A long string of college degrees was absent. she didn't have a rich husband. She was a widow. Her family background was not impressive. But she came from a good American family. Her father was a barber. And she started to earn her own money early in life.

Just what did she have that other women who have all the above lacks do not have? She possessed an alert mind and a keen interest in everything about her. A pleasing personality, she liked to meet people. She could work hard, too. She turn mere acquaintances into close friends. You can sense that she was expressing her best potentials in her relations with other people.

People who work at keeping their public relations in hand -- whether they know it or not -- always stand out from the crowd. I recall hearing of a certain sales girl from several of my students and clients who were unknown to each other. Even so, they all spoke highly of this wonderful girl. They said if I ever went in Blank store to be sure and ask for her.

Truth is, at that time I seldom went shopping for clothes as I had a client who was a dress designer, who made all my clothes. But after hearing about this girl from several sources. I began to think she had something out of the ordinary to impress folks so strongly with her personality.

One day I took an extra trip and went to Blank's store. I asked for that sales girl. She introduced herself and asked my name. I knew from what others have told me that she would call me by name when I went back to that store.

She took her time and talked with me about the type of purchase I had in mind. Instead of rushing about and saying, "This is just your type. why don't you try it on!" or some such thing, she listened to me after asking what I had in mind. This way she was not wasting her time or the customer's either.

She had a subtle yet persuasive way of letting you know that the type that attracts your eye was not right for you. She didn't insult or abruptly give this information. Indirectly she would talk up the good points rather than the faults. In this way the customer was politely lead to choose her right type. She took a great deal of time assisting the customer make her decision .

She treated every customer with as much interest. Some of her coworkers fell all over themselves to wait on the mink-sheathed women. But they were not remembered like our favorite girl, who was certainly doing a splendid job on her public relations.

By keeping her public relations in hand, this sales girl was building happiness patterns for the future. Not only that, many kind absent treatments reached her from her satisfied customers.

Chapter 3

LOCATING HOROSCOPE HOUSES

An accurate astrological interpretation demands a birth chart calculated for the year, month, day and hour at the place of birth of the person. Then a consideration of four astrological factors forms the base from which guidelines for successful living can be found.

The basic four include: 1) The planets, which are the chief source of astrological energy and map the desires in the subconscious mind. 2) The zodiacal signs, which map the motivation behind specific desires. 3) The aspects, which are combinations of planets (subconscious urges) and map the various complexes in the person's makeup. 4) The houses, which picture the departments of life that are affected by the desires (planets) through their motivation (sign association) and combinations (aspects). In this chapter we will consider the last of the basic four, the houses.

Perhaps the most difficult conception for the beginner to realize is that the houses are stationary. They remain the same from the cradle to the grave. The other basic factors have motion. Regardless of how other factors break and form, the houses maintain the same position. This is due to the fact that the planets in the sky are viewed from a specific place on earth.

One of my correspondence students wrote asking "Where is my second house? I was born so-and-so." The letter writer did not understand the house cusp positions. In all charts, the cusp of the second house is below the first house. Several people may have different signs on that cusp and different planets located in the signs, but the second house is always found in the same place in all charts.

WE LOCATE THE HOUSES

If you do not happen to have a printed horoscope blank handy, it is suggested that you draw one so that the following information can be more readily understood.

On a blank paper, preferably 8" by 11", draw a circle. Make it at least six inches across, the bigger the better. Then you can make notes on it for future study. As if the circle were a pie, divide it into twelve equal "pieces" by drawing first a line across from one side to the other, then another line from the top to the bottom.

That gives you four equal divisions, called quadrants. Each quadrant embraces three houses. Therefore, we next divide each one by two more lines to give three spaces (houses) in each quadrant. When all have been drawn, we have twelve lines (cusps) which meet at the center. The spaces in between are the houses of the horoscope.

At the line that extends furthest to the left, write Ascendant. This is the starting point. The Ascendant is always the first house cusp, and the space just below it is the first house. In that space at the center of the wheel, write "1". Going down to the next space, write "2". Continue around the wheel counter clockwise until you have numbered all twelve houses. As you read the information, you can jot down notes in each house space and you will have a handy diagram for future reference.

Quaternary approach brings method to the study of the horoscope houses. That is, we consider house meanings in four ways. (1) Each house as a unit. (2) the duality of the houses. (3) Houses as a trinity. And (4) Houses in quaternary relationship.

DUAL RELATIONSHIP

In general, the six houses above the horizon (represented by the horizontal line through the center of the chart) tend to give the things they map easy expression. Often the activities receive more recognition. the six houses below the horizon map trends which tend to develop in ways which do not receive as much recognition. However, in synthesizing the whole chart, it is possible to change this general trend if other factors are present.

Next, we consider the number of planets East and West. The vertical line through the middle of the chart divides the houses. The houses to the left are East. Activities mapped by these houses depend more or less upon the person's initiative, for then he has the ability to a certain extent for shaping the course of his actions.

The activities of the western houses (to the right of the middle line) are more dependent upon the actions of others and outside factors. That is, the person seems to have less ability for molding life's pathway. These are general trends which may be modified by a complete synthesis of the chart.

TRINITIES

The twelve houses fall into four trinities (3x4 equals 12.).

The Life Trinity contains the first, fifth and ninth houses. Activities in these three departments of life are intimately tied in with life itself. The first house maps the person's constitution and vitality in general. The fifth house pictures the life of the children (physical and mental). The ninth house portrays his general attitude toward religion and philosophy.

The Psychic Trinity embraces the fourth, eighth and twelfth houses. The fourth house maps the home, inherited tendencies and conditions in transition. The eighth house rules death, inheritance and relations with those who have passed to the next plane. The twelfth house pictures sorrows as well as trends for spiritual adjustment.

The Wealth Trinity is composed of the second, sixth and tenth houses. These houses are important from the business angle. The second house maps the personal property and money, as well as the person's idea of positions (which in some cases may not be money at all). The sixth house shows the work or employees. The tenth house rules the job itself and the honor attached to it.

The Association Trinity includes the third, seventh and eleventh

11

houses. All of them deal with people. The third pictures relatives in general, but specifically brothers and sisters, and neighbors. The seventh portrays the partner, marriage or other people in general. The eleventh house maps friends, counselors, and well-wishers.

QUATERNARY RELATIONSHIP

Observation and experimentation have revealed that some houses are stronger, that is, have more volume than others. In the quaternary relationship we consider volume, which is something aside from harmony or discord. If we strike the note C on a piano keyboard with great force, the loud tone is comparable to the **Angular Houses,** which embrace the first, fourth, seventh and tenth house, or the first house of each quadrant of the chart. They express the strongest volume.

Now should we play the keyboard G with an ordinary touch, it would be comparable to the **Succedent Houses,** that is, it would be moderate in volume. The Succedent Houses are the second, fifth, eighth, and eleventh.

Before pressing the note G, if we press down the soft pedal of the piano, the resulting tone would be weak. This is comparable to the **Cadent Houses,** Which are third, sixth, ninth and twelfth. The volume is weak.

Another quaternary relationship is called the Societies. The **Personal Houses** embrace the twelfth, first, second and third houses. These houses concern the personal action behind the scenes, (12) the personal body, (1) personal property (2) and the personal thoughts (3).

If many planets appear in this category, the individual trends to have a personal, outlook and his main interest and action is focussed in that direction.

The **Companionship Houses** include the fourth, fifth, sixth and seventh houses. Here the interest is outside of self and extended to others. The person with many planets in this society gets companionship in the home (4), with children (5), servants (6), partners and public general (7). He likes pleasures. In order to be happy he needs and desires association with other people.

The **Public Houses** are the eighth, ninth, tenth and eleventh. All of these houses embrace events which gain public recognition. Public life is marked by deaths, legacies (8), publicly expressed opinion (9), reputation, credit (10) and friends (11). A person having a chart with many clients The Public Houses are the eighth, ninth and tenth and eleventh. All of these houses embrace events which gain public recognition. Public life is marked by deaths, legacies, publicly expressed opinion, reputation, credit and friends. A person having a chart with many planets in this society usually comes before the public and his efforts are easily recognized.

The fourth approach of classifying the houses is to study the individual meaning of each house of the horoscope, considering the house as a unit. Here we include all factors under the rule of each house. Many text books give these things that each house governs. In the book *Profit by Electional Astrology* * many charts are presented in groups according to the house that rules the chief topic of each chapter.

*D.C. Doane. AFA. Tempe Az. 1990

Chapter 4

ZODIACAL SIGNS AND ADAPTABILITY

Mrs. Thorne had just returned from attending her 25th class reunion. She told us the thing that amazed her most was how very little her classmates had changed in the last twenty-five years. Even though they had all changed in looks, their personalities were very much the same. There was Vera. She had always wanted to be the center of attention. Today she was holding true to the old pattern still figuring out ways of getting attention. Liza had always been calm, cool and collected. She still was. In fact, she was a well-poised woman. Millie had been the class grind. She was still taking life seriously. The flighty girls were still running around in circles.

In describing her reunion, Mrs. Thorne said she was truly amazed at the "girls". So she put herself through a drilling analysis to try harder to erase some of her own least desirable traits. She said her visit had convinced her that as we grow older, these undesirable traits become more and more crystallized into our personalities. She had discovered a universal truth. Time doesn't change us, for we have a change ourselves.

She was right. Time resulted only in the flighty girls becoming more neurotic. The attention-getters became more selfish. The unhappy girls continued to lament their conditions. The solution to all of these conditions is to make a change in the character traits.

Change is the most certain thing in the world. Our bodies change every day as we cast off the old tissues and build new ones through metabolism. The circumstances we live under are also changing from day to day. Therefore the person who gets the most out of life is always adaptable.

Webster defines *adaptable* as "that which can be adapted or can easily adapt itself". In other words, flexibility of character is needed as we adjust to the day to day stresses and strains we are bound to experience. How we resist or bend with the life current in each instance molds our character. Thus the ability to change and adjust is a great asset in fashioning oneself a happy life.

To find out how adaptable you are, here are a few general questions with which to test yourself. The more "no" answers you can give, the more adaptable you are.

1. Does it worry you if others have opinions different than your own.?
2. Are you facing the future with confidence, feeling ready to take the next step in life regardless of what it is?
3. Does your happiness depend entirely upon having one certain person near you at all times?
4. Is your conversation turning more and more to the "good old days"?
5. Are you still telling the same stories and talking about the same experiences that you were last year?

The signs of the zodiac that are emphasized in your natal horoscope will give a clue to your own motivation and to whether it will help or hinder you in adapting to new conditions in your environment. If negative indications appear there, directed thinking and induced emotions of a specific antidotal type can act as corrective measures.

When establishing the strong trends in character, we look to the position of the Sun which maps the most deep-seated trends in the person's makeup, the Moon which rules the mentality and the Ascendant which indicates the personality. In addition, should we find a number of planets located in one sign of the zodiac, that sign is an important indicant to the motivation of the person's total behavior pattern.

If we look at physical matter, we find that it exists in three states of being: gas, liquid or solid. We can compare the signs of the zodiac to these three states of being, and this association brings a meaningful interpretation to each sign. The signs are categorized three ways: The Cardinal (Movable) Signs, the Fixed Signs, and the Mutable (Common) Signs.

The Cardinal group embraces Aries, Cancer, Libra and Capricorn. You will notice there is a sign from each element -- fire, water, air and earth respectively. These signs express the nature of its element in its highest state of activity. Thus Aries is the most active fire sign, Cancer is the most active water sign, Libra is the most active air sign, and Capricorn is the most active earth sign.

When matter is found in the gaseous state -- as compared with a solid or a liquid -- it possesses different and more active qualities. The correspondence is seen also in the Cardinal signs. People with a Cardinal emphasis in their horoscopes are more active, changeable and have more energy to spend than the natives of the other signs. They are likened to gas, which generates power and goes into places where other types of matter cannot enter.

In much the same manner people whose charts emphasize the Cardinal signs are the initiators. They rush forth to blaze new trails. However, each sign signifies a pioneering in its own particular nature: Aries for enterprises and adventure; Cancer for homes and food; Libra for literature, arts and society; and Capricorn for business and industry.

Falling into the Fixed group are Taurus, Leo, Scorpio and Aquarius. Just as in physical matter where there is a solid state of being which is unyielding and rigid, these signs express each of the four elements in their lowest state of activity. Taurus is the least active of the earth signs, Leo is the least active fire sign, Scorpio is the least active water sign, and Aquarius is the least active air sign. They are the most unchanging of the particular elements they represent.

Just as solid matter finds difficulty in altering its form or placement, so do people with a horoscope that emphasizes the Fixed group dislike to alter their environment and their customary trends of thinking. They have strong endurance and can keep a thing for a long time. They will plod persistently until a job is completed. They have a great resistance to all kinds of pressure which might be brought to bear.

Gemini, Virgo, Sagittarius and Pisces are the signs which make up the Mutable group. These signs express the four different elements in a medium state of activity. Comparable to matter in a liquid state, the yielding and adaptability is outstanding.

This group is a happy medium between the aggressive and the extremely active Cardinal signs and the firm and unyielding Fixed signs. The gas which typifies the pioneer can enter any little opening, but the liquid which symbolizes the Mutable group depends upon a trail that has been blazed. Once a trail or new channel has been blazed, the Mutable groups will follow the line of least resistance and flow into it without any trouble.

Thus we see that in general the Cardinal group take the aggressive action and bring out the new and untried, then the Mutable group perfect the details and plod on to finish the job.

That is a clue to adaptability. If we note a strong Fixed accent in the chart then we can look into thoughts, feelings and actions to see if we are becoming stubborn in regard to new trends. That condition can overtake anyone with prior notice. Therefore, if the chart maps such a condition, the person should check his own thoughts, feelings and actions for clues.

In the case of a strong emphasis in the Mutable group, we should investigate the thoughts, feelings and actions to insure that the personal energies are not wasted in the daily business of adjusting to the conditions of life.

If the emphasized symbolism falls in the Cardinal group, we need to see if we are pouring out too much energy, thus draining the vital life force which enables us to contribute our utmost to the family and society, even at the same time we are adapting our way to happiness.

17

Chapter 5

A HAPPY HOME

Sally and Jack Blake had a charming home. The moment you stepped into the door, the living-room seemed to beckon "Come on in, folks, and have a chair!"

After your first impression you realize that their home is not all decorated in the last word of fashion. No, there is something more than just physical decoration that goes into the makeup of their charming home. The vibration throughout is one of peace and harmony.

Anyone who is at all sensitive to vibrations can tell when a fight has been raging or a tension is afloat as they enter a room. Even though many people do not realize it, they tune in on these vibrations almost everyday of their lives.

If they are feeling a big negative, the contact emphasizes the discord within them. Yet, if they are feeling cheerful, their mood is somewhat dampened at the contact, unless the mood is extremely high and intense. If the mood is intensely polarized on a high plane, no lower vibrations can get in and drag the spirit down the emotional ladder.

Sally and Jack are occult students. They take a keen interest in imponderable forces. They have been working with their thoughts and feelings, trying to keep them expressing on a high level, so they will at all times stimulate the harmony in their relationship with each other. This, in turn, permeates their home and any environment in which they find themselves with a harmonious vibration.

They have been successful in doing just that. When you enter their home, you can feel it. You always get an uplifting feeling when you visit them as their house emanates blessings to all comers.

Perhaps the first point in considering a home is that of locality. It is true that most of us have to make do with what we have. However, if the chance comes which will enable us to select a proper location, how should we go about it?

Thankfully not everyone desires the same environment. The surroundings which are best for each person is mapped by the zodiacal sign in which the best planet is located in his birth chart. One method in making this determination is by consulting a Cosmodyne Report.* If the consideration involves a family, the best influence reflected by all birth charts should be chosen.

There is a wide variety of different localities in which to live. Some people like the heights, some the lowlands. Some the bustle of the city, others the calm of the country. Here, briefly, are the specific environments for each zodiacal sign.

Aries: A hot, dry climate, thinly settled, moderately high and rugged. Taurus: A cold climate. Low, level country without brush or woods. Gemini: A temperate climate, thickly settled. A city or town, moderately high where the wind blows. Grass, small trees and shrubs on rolling land.

Cancer: A wet, cool climate, along the ocean beach or where active streams flow. Rich, sandy soil. Leo: A hot, dry climate, rather low with level plains, tending to desert conditions. Land unkempt or used for recreational purposes, such as near golf courses, etc. Virgo: A cold, climate with moderate rainfall, moderately elevated. Land which is used for orchards, crops and grain fields.

Libra: A temperate climate, high and dry. Towns and villages rather thickly settled. Scorpio: A damp, sultry climate, more low than high, away from the ocean in a valley. Land with bogs, swamps, muddy ground and hot springs. Sagittarius: A hot, dry climate in mountainous country, rather high. Wooded land.

* *How to Read Cosmodynes,* D. C. Doane. AFA. Tempe AZ. 1974.

19

Capricorn: A cold climate with a fair amount of snowfall, well up into the rugged mountains. Mining land, covered with rocks and brush, poor soil.
Aquarius: A temperate climate. Land being neither high nor low, changeable weather. Thickly settled, such as a city. Land chiefly used for habitation.
Pisces: A cool, rainy, foggy climate. Moderately low and broken up land. Plot shut in by hills. Land near water, rivers, lakes or hot springs.

After selecting the location and environment, we are ready to acquire a house. Here again, the selection is an individual matter. If possible, a house should be planned about the activities and temperaments of those who will occupy it. In this manner, the greatest amount of comfort and functional ease will be assured.

If one of the family works at a job which soils the hands and clothes, then, he will feel uncomfortable walking into a room furnished all in white. He will feel more at ease with a den or recreation room where he can go to relax and catch his breath before slicking up for dinner. Then home will be a comfortable place for him.

Sometimes folks become overzealous in their attitude toward cleanliness. Unless this approach is guarded against, a person can become a slave, instead of an occupant, in his own house. A spot of dirt on the living room rug will mean more to him than the happiness and relaxation of the family.

One of my neighbors had actually driven her children from home with just such an attitude. She wondered why they were always out away from home. She didn't stop to consider that she had forbade them to invite their playmates into the house "because it would dirty up the place."

On the other hand, another woman keeps her children at home and happily interested there by having all the kids in the neighborhood over for snacks and fun after school. There is plenty of freedom of action here. You feel no restraint whatever. Her house is truly a home, not just a place to sleep and run from. It has that lived-in feeling.

If a happy home is your objective you have to consider common things. One is stuffiness in the air. Check the circulation frequently. Be sure chairs are comfortable. Try to minimize excessive noise in a subtle way. If these and similar things are kept in order, many of the psychological stresses have little chance to grow into discord. Members of the family will not seek comfort and entertainment outside the home exclusively.

Every member of the family should be subtly encouraged to take an unselfish interest in the home, no matter what age. Happy people thrive on sparkle, movement and a change, as well as periods of calm reflection and restfulness.

In addition to physical comforts and conveniences, mental stimulation is important. Good books and periodicals will be found in the happy home. Entertainment, too, upon occasion. Music aids in helping to vitalize and maintain the happy vibration.

All of the foregoing elements are easy to obtain, in a manner of speaking. But the most important attribute for a happy home is for all family members to realize that each one of them has different habit systems (shown by their horoscopes) and thus reacts differently to various stimulation.

Whenever personalities clash and the individuals cannot seem to resolve the conflict, that is the time to consult a certified astrologer for explanations and guidance. Write for counselor contacts to: Professional Astrologers, Inc., 1020 Tenth Street, Sacramento CA 95814, or the American Federation of Astrologers, Inc., P O Box 22040, Tempe AZ 85285-2040.

Ripples of discord begin to develop when Joan is moody with thoughts a million miles away. Her brother speaks to her in an abrupt manner. Joan gets upset because he disturbed her reverie. She should be made to understand that cooperation is the most important trait for building a happy home. Her brother should be made to understand the respect for other people's feelings. Bickering, outbursts of anger, nagging, and the like cause a lot of unpleasantness for others.

Of course, the person who is poised and pleasant all the time is a rare individual. However, every member of the family can work out his own negative kinks with the aid of astrology. Then he will be able to contribute more peaceful vibrations to the home and insure happiness.

Chapter 6

THE "MYSTERIOUS" EIGHTH HOUSE

I would like to direct this chapter to beginning students, who often find it difficult reading the eighth house. Sure, it is said to rule death. That's the end of life. But we are alive, so let's think of what else the eighth house rules.

Wait a minute! I can't skip over death as quickly as that. After all, it is a part of life. However, no ethical astrologer will discuss death with a client.

For years when anyone was asked, "What does the eighth house stand for?" invariably the answer rolled off the tongue, "Death, debts, and taxes."

Let's look at debts. What kind of debts? The eighth house maps the money the native owes others as well as the money owed him. So it also governs loans, as well as trust funds, deeds, fiduciaries, and stock equity that pays dividends out of profits. Any type of interest is also pictured, whether from Certificate of Deposits, bank accounts, bonds, stocks, etc. fall under eighth house rule.

Taxes? All kind of taxes: Federal, state, city, sales, income, etc. These fall under rule of the eighth.

Joint finances are eighth house. That is, the combined funds of husband and wife, or business partners. It is the partner's income and also corporate funds. In a sale, it represents the other fellow's ability to pay.

If the person is in business, the seventh house rules his customers or clients, and the eighth indicates their ability to pay for services that the native provides.

22

Some books say that the eighth house rules sex. In my research I have found that the fifth house rules sex. A little research with case history related to birth horoscopes can speedily prove that.

I imagine that some students feel that sex is ruled by the eighth house because in a natural wheel (where Aries appears on the Ascendant and the rest of the signs follow in a counter-clockwise direction) Scorpio falls on the eighth cusp. However, when we cast a chart precisely for the birth hour, Scorpio rarely appears on the eighth cusp. This is due to Aries being the sign of shortest Ascension (on the horizon-first cusp).

On the other hand, I go along with the eighth house ruling regeneration. This could refer to the regeneration of body chemistry, regeneration of thoughts, etc. In these instances, there is a death of sort; the death of something old, out of which emerges the birth of something new.

Here the implication is not something brand new but rather the old is blended with a new face -- a transmutation has taken place. It is as if a cyclic manifestation evolves higher and higher. Refined and more refined. This is nothing whatever to do with a past life or a next life. The birth chart merely shows potential energy releases from the cradle to the grave.

Insurance comes under this house. These days insurance is certainly a greater part of life than death. How the native will benefit or lose financially through activities associated with insurance will be shown when progressions of the planets stimulate the eighth house rulers. The map also points to how he will probably handle these energy patterns in his personal life.

Escrow also comes into the eighth house area. When you buy or sell a house or are involved in real estate transactions, the eighth house, as well as the fourth house (property), should be considered in delineating a chart.

A savings account which draws interest from a bank or a savings and loan company is an eighth house matter. Other people are using your money and paying you for the privilege.

Credit purchases, where you are charged interest, come under this rule, because ownership remains in the hands of the seller until payment is completed. In fact, all credit buying and selling is eighth house.

This is also a psychic house (along with houses four and twelve). However, I have not entered this area for this book as these thoughts are geared to physical, day-to-day living on the material plane. However, in passing it should be pointed out that this house rules discarnate souls -- those who have passed to the next plane.

Chapter 7

FIND FRIENDS IN YOUR HOROSCOPE

Sally Major was a fetching and attractive girl. I met her while on a business trip to a small town. As I stayed there several weeks, I had a chance to become well acquainted with Sally. She was secretary to the Town Mayor. In that position her personality was a great asset.

Being interested in astrology and its relation to her friendliness, I asked her for her birth data. In her chart the eleventh house ruling friends showed the planet Jupiter, which was trining (a luck aspect) to another aspect, a conjunction of Venus and the Moon. These aspects certainly reflected her charming manner.

Long ago it was proved to me that aspects alone will not tell the complete story. I made a study of Sally's background the way she conducted herself. She didn't know I was doing so. But I had ample opportunity to find out these things through her friends who were always willing to confide to me the nice gestures Sally was always doing on the quiet. she never seemed to ask for credit or recognition.

When judging astrological patterns we need to take in account the person's conditioning energy. Sally came from a broken home. However, her maiden aunt had raised her and given her a good education. She encouraged Sally to read good books to improve herself and a knowledge of people and the world.

It was in this manner that she became interested in psychology. She said she devoured all the little self-help books she could find. Yet, she had never investigated astrology. Before I left town, I introduced her to this fascinating and helpful study. To this day I receive notes telling of her progress how her studies have helped her in all ways.

Sally has the knack of making, keeping and being a friend. My sleuthing turned up some interesting angles. They are, in fact, what has formed her conditioning energy. In reading a horoscope, it is absolutely essential to know the native's conditioning energy. That energy is the sum total of all past experiences from which every thought, feeling and action is colored. when this conditioning of a person is taken into account, the interpretation gives a well-rounded index of that person.

Books on how to have friends advise you to compliment people to make them feel good. There is a particular aspect of such conduct that demands consideration. It can be summed up in the question: "Is the compliment of praise sincere, or is it just plain flattery?"

There are many more people than most of us realize who have a markedly developed extrasensory perception in regards to what is said about them. They can instinctively pick up, or tune into, the motive behind the compliment. If the remark is only flattery, chances are that the comment does more to alienate the person than to win him over as a friend.

Apparently, Sally was not guilty of giving flattery. There was one outstanding thing in her favor. When she met a person for the first time, she did not gush over him and compliment him first thing. She had what might be called a good psychological delaying action. After the conversation has progressed a bit, then she would subtly bring in a compliment. Because the first impact of the meeting had worn off, the other person was in a receptive mood to appreciate the comment.

She was a natural human gardener in that she planted seeds of harmony. If she was in a position to do so, she always let a person know of some nice comment a third person had remarked about him. The chain of harmony passed between the three persons, and no doubt the feeling of goodness was transmitted to others. Thus the garden of harmony grew and grew.

As she went about her work and play in that town, she could be likened to a radio station broadcasting harmonious programs, which brought a feeling of well-being and happiness to all who tuned in on her wave length. The Police Chief outdid himself in describing her help to others. He emphasized the fact that she seemed to know when a compliment or a word of praise would do the most good. At times when a person was feeling blue or low, she went right ahead and gave them a lift. When a person seemed to be in good spirits, she was not so apt to give praise or encouragement. Then she engaged in a lively and humorous conversation. Such an approach vitalized the already present spirit of good will.

In that town, all the executive offices, as well as the jail, were housed in the Town Hall. Sally's desk was in the Mayor's office, so she was handy to the jail. Although they seldom had prisoners there, when they did she always made it a point to visit the occupants. Even here she spread her good will and cheer. The chief said he had more than once caught her heading down the hall toward the jail with a steaming pot of coffee.

One evening at a church social some ladies remarked about Sally's friendly and helpful disposition. One woman in particular seemed to put her finger on an important point. She was talking about how Sally did favors.

She said that when you were on the receiving end of one of her favors, you never felt as if you had to pay her back in some way. She had the gift of giving and doing things for others in a sincere manner. She achieved that graciousness which does not call for a favor in return. Also, she never talked or bragged about the favors she had given others. She just went about her good deeds in a quiet manner. So she kept right on winning friends and charming others. Others never noticed that she had to carry a heavy brace on her leg.

Regardless of what particular aspects we have in our horoscopes, it seems as if Sally's attitude would be a good one to adopt. But in addition, we can take corrective steps, if need be, to transmute any discordant trends which might appear in the chart.

The kind of friends attracted, the influence they tend to have upon our lives, and our attitude towards friends are indicated by the eleventh house in the birth chart. The zodiacal sign on the cusp of that house, the planets located in it and any planets ruling the cusp sign (and perhaps an intercepted sign), and their aspects will portray the trend. After synthesizing these factors and an

Positive Benefits of Astrology

unfavorable trend is found, then we can do something about it by practicing *Mental Alchemy.**

Briefly, here are the trends symbolized by the ten planets as each appears in the eleventh house of friends. The Sun: people in authority, employers, male sex in general. Moon: people from all walks of life, especially females. Mercury: studious, literary and other types. Venus: artists, pleasure loving and social people and the refined type. Mars: aggressive, active types, doctors, mechanics, etc. Jupiter: generous and cheerful types, professionals. Saturn: older, serious types, businessmen. Uranus: progressive, unconventional and ingenious types. Neptune: dreamy, imaginative types and psychics. Pluto: groups of people, intense types, charitable.

As an example, Henry Ford had Jupiter in the eleventh house of his natal chart. It was well aspected. He benefitted immensely from influential friends. His Jupiter was sextile (opportunity aspect) Mars in the ninth house indicating his close friendship with John Burroughs, the writer. The ninth house position maps the writer. His friendship with Harvey Firestone and George Eastman, both manufacturers, is portrayed by the planet Mars.

Henry Ford's Jupiter was also trine Uranus in the seventh house of his natal chart, indicating his friendship with Thomas A Edison, the inventor (Uranus). Thus the ruling planet of his eleventh house and its aspects gave a picture of the type of friends attracted into Henry Ford's life.

*C.C. Zain. The Church of Light, Inc. Los Angeles CA. 1936

Chapter 8

MAKE YOUR CONVERSATION COLORFUL

"Words are but shadows of actions." - Plutarch

There are a lot of things about color which at first seem strange. Color can be closely associated with the pattern of life and a reflection of the symbols in a horoscope. Thoughts, moods, and emotions are keyed to colors. Through a study of *Astrological Signatures**, the significance of color is revealed.

It wouldn't be at all unusual if you did not recognize the coat-of-arms of the King of Siam or the signature of an Egyptian princess. Yet to a person familiar with the language, history, and customs of these respective countries, your ignorance would lower you somewhat in his social scale. That is so because language is a community affair, which rests upon a given social system having its own traditions.

Much the same may be said for the one who is unfamiliar with the language of the stars. However, we who are familiar with the zodiac, the planets and the birth chart recognize this universal language. We also recognize the law of astrological signatures, where each planetary family is said to have rule over things of a like influence.

Every object and certain groups of objects, as well as thoughts which we contact, have a radiating energy which vibrates to a certain tone or

*C.C. Zain. The Church of Light, Inc. Los Angeles CA. 1925

octave of this basic keytone. The Law of Affinity, like attracts like, works with all centers of energy regardless if it emanates from a thought number or what have you.

Plutarch stated that words are but the shadows of actions. In dealing with planetary trends in colorful conversation, we must look to the substance which casts the shadow. So our first problem is to establish the colors and basic keytones with their equivalents in the planetary families.

Including the Sun and Moon as such, even though they are luminaries, there are seven basic planets which correspond to the seven basic musical notes of the scale and to the seven basic colors of the rainbow. Furthermore, each planet corresponds to a basic urge in the subconscious mind. While the planets are not the cause of these thought-families embracing a subconscious urge, the energy they radiate is of a similar keytone and frequency.

TABLE OF CORRESPONDENCES

Planet	Music	Color	Urge
Mars	C	Red	Aggressive
Sun	D	Orange	Power
Venus	E	Yellow	Social
Moon	F	Green	Domestic
Saturn	G	Blue	Safety
Jupiter	A	Purple	Religious
Mercury	B	Violet	Intellectual

You have no doubt noticed how colorful phrases make an impact upon the sensibilities. It is a powerful associative device, and the appeal is primarily to the emotions. There is much richness of suggestion in words. Usually the emphasis is not placed upon literal meaning but upon figurative phrases which quicken the feelings.

Some Authorities estimate the bulk of the English vocabulary to embrace about two million terms and meanings. Thus we can easily see that expression is unlimited. A study of color and its relation to words and phrases shows two manifestations. (1) It produces overtones, and (2) it is either pleasurable or painful. These trends are seen when associating certain phrases or words with a planetary family as expressed through a subconscious urge in the mind of man.

Mars corresponds to the color red and to the Aggressive Urge in the subconscious mind. Red is the passionate and ardent hue of the spectrum, marking love and hatred, compassion and war, the saint and the sinner, patriotism, and anarchy. All great emotions, great extremes, heroic or base, seem to be associated with red.

It is the symbol of courage, cruelty, bloodshed, martyrdom, danger, justice, health. Its usage in the extreme may be found in "red-light district" (a district in which disorderly resorts, often indicated by a red light, are frequent) and in Red Cross (a national society for reliving suffering in war and calamity).

Man must paint the town red, he sees red when his anger is aroused, his newspaper is filled with red-hot news, he is the victim of red tape, he hears politicians rant about the Reds, he has red letter days, and when he is broke he is in the red and hasn't a red cent to his name. He attends pink teas, and he gazes through rose-colored glasses for a happy if unreal glimpse of life.

The Sun corresponds to the color orange and to the Power Urges in the subconscious mind. Orange is the kingly color of the spectrum, ranging in hue from reddish red-yellow to red-yellow. It is the binding force between the Aggressive Urges (red) and the Social Urges (yellow). These two urges correspond to Mars and Venus, the planets having rule over sex. Therefore it is not at all surprising to find the orange blossom prominently associated with the wedding ritual.

31

Positive Benefits of Astrology

The Golden wedding represents a half century of wedded union. In tracing the origin of the word orange, we find it connected with the old French AUR, meaning gold. Power is associated with gold, and the Sun corresponds to the gold of the alchemists. History tells of the Golden Age, a period of great prosperity and progress, the flowering of civilization and art.

We have prices adjusted to a gold standard (power). Man has his golden (precious) hours, he lives by the Golden Rule (doing to others as he would have them do to him), and if he violates the rule, he is a gold-bricker.

Venus corresponds to the color yellow and to the Social Urges in the subconscious mind. Yellow is the color of the spectrum which has the most attractive qualities. In experimental psychology, it was found to be the color most often recognized in color-tests. Therefore, we would expect it to be extremely sensitive and potent. This may be the reason for its negative use in language, which is often anti-social and directed to the emotions (Venus).

Man refers to a scoundrel as a yellow dog, he calls a coward yellow, the timid person has a yellow streak, or he may have *"a jaundiced humor"*, which means he is jealous. The most sensitive spot on the human retina is called the yellow spot.

As an experiment in printing, a New York newspaper ran a picture of a child in a yellow dress. This was followed shortly by a newspaper headed: *"The Yellow Press Is For War With Spain At All Costs"* (1898). Since then yellow has become a symbol of sensational journalism.

The Moon corresponds to the color green and to the Domestic Urges in the subconscious mind. Green is synonymous with nature and growth. It lacks troublesome, holy, or profane qualities. Therefore, it is not a fertile source of colloquialism like the rest of the spectrum. It is akin to mother, home and hearth. It at once represents the picture of new growth, following a period of gestation. The green-horn is a raw, inexperienced person, and the greener is an inexperienced worker. Green refers to the unripened and immature.

When his emotions (Moon) are attacked, man becomes green-eyed (based by jealousy). Many tales have been related about the Green Dragon of jealousy and fear. Man exchanges green-backs, the fluid of our economical system, and he looks back upon green (full of life and vigor) memories.

Saturn corresponds to the color blue and to the Safety Urges in the subconscious mind. Just as Saturn is the father of experience, the color blue is indispensable in its relation to colorful phrases. At one time or another man has had the thought "I feel blue". The illusion to blue ties in with dejection, despair, restriction, privation and obstacle, but in the absence of these clouds of negativism the skies are blue.

In the past century many expressions came into being and embraced these qualities. There were the Blue Laws (said to have been bound in blue covers), blue funk for hysteria and panic, blue gloom for the reformer. The first day back to school or to work became blue Monday. Man would yell blue murder and curse the air blue.

The Blue-blood was one whose ancestry and blood were nor vulgar, that is, red (Mars) like that of the mob. The blue stocking was one well cultivated in intellect but without much compassion (red).

Jupiter corresponds to the color purple and to the Religious Urges in the subconscious mind. Purple is the regal, imperial, proud hue of the spectrum, marking the professionals and religious potentates. Roman emperors wore robes of this color to emblemize their rank and authority. In the ritualistic ceremonies of many religions we find purple to be a prominent color in the settings and furnishings of the environment.

The Mauve Decade was an era when people were neither red (Mars) nor blue (Saturn), but a combination of the two. This balance of Mars and Saturn is likened to the judge, who is ruled by Jupiter.

Purple also expresses as priggishness, which is a form of pride often mapped in the horoscope by an afflicted Jupiter, and at times it manifests as purple rage. A purple time expressed an Englishman's conception of a happy affair, which was attended by those born to the purple, meaning of wealth or royalty.

Mercury corresponds to the color violet and to the Intellectual Urges in the subconscious mind. Violet is the shortest ray in the visible spectrum. Higher frequencies cannot be captured and interpreted by the physical eye. Just as Mercury, the winged messenger of the gods, is vacillating, the color violet has never quite been captured by colloquialism.

The allusion to violet is synonymous with mental ability, reason, intuition, perception, and expression. In healing the violet ray is used for its penetrative purposes. Man uses a mercury-vapor lamp which emits a light rich in actinis and ultra-violet rays. The shrinking violet ties in with the short rays of the color.

Mercury's duality is found in a myriad of common expressions such as fork in tongue, out of both sides of his mouth, and other volatile phrases. The mercurial person is endowed with swiftness, cleverness and eloquence.

Chapter 9

YOUR JEWEL IN THE ZODIAC

From the earliest ages jewels have held a powerful attraction for man. They have been the causes of war, the gifts of kings, and the influence concerned with arts, manners, and customs, which are strange, romantic and fascinating. Their symbolism and sentiment permeate literature. The known history of some notable gems covers a period of time longer than the history of modern nations.

Tradition, passed from generation to generation, asserts that special stones, gems, or metals bring good luck when worn by certain people. Unlike a talisman, to which vibrations must be inculcated, the gem has an inherent vibratory rate of its own. This occult property was taken on faith until the present century, when scientists proved conclusively that gems may be alive, asleep, or even dead. There is intelligence to a degree present.

Ancient initiates believed that each gem was an entity having subjective intelligence, about which was built the crystalline physical form. They also found that coral, pearls, and amber, even though not occupied by some intelligences, had an intense vibratory quality which was transferred to the wearer.

A close rapport is suppose to take place between the subjective intelligence of the gem and the subconscious mind of the wearer if the vibratory rate is sympathetic. As this intelligence functions on the astral plane, it is sensitive to coming events and is able to warn the wearer of danger or to impress the subconscious mind to take advantage of an opportunity.

On the other hand, if the vibratory rate is antagonistic to the wearer, he is impressed to take actions which lead him into danger and place a bar to successful living. All of which points to the tradition that some gems have a *good* influence and some have a *bad* influence. In themselves they are neither good nor bad. The influence is determined in terms of the particular centers of harmony or discord stimulated within the subconscious mind of the person wearing the jewel.

The road-map to successful living is the individual birth chart, which pictures in zodiacal symbolism the harmonious and discordant factors within the person. The ancients claimed that to be beneficial a gem must be alive and should be selected with reference to the horoscope.

Every planetary position in the chart corresponds to an energy-center in the astral body (or subconscious mind). This center has the same vibratory rate as the planet. The harmonious centers predispose to attract good fortune, and the discordant centers tend to attract misfortune into the life. Therefore, we find that the type of conditions or events drawn from the environment rely upon the harmony or discord of the energy-centers (mapped by planets), if nothing is done to change it.

It is possible to determine which planet in the natal chart is the best (most harmonious), the worst (most afflicted), or the dominant (most powerful or prominent). So with the best, worst and dominant zodiacal sign (motivation) and house (department of life).

Furthermore, any one of these various focal points may be emphasized to a certain extent by wearing the jewel of a corresponding vibratory rate.

In light of that information, we can indeed see the importance of stimulating centers which will help us to attract our chosen goals. In general, however, a gem selected to correspond to your best planet will be most effective in assisting you to attain successful living.

Man attracts to himself from without that which corresponds to the man within. Gems have proven to be one of the objects to intensify the inner centers. The activities of the harmonious centers in the astral body can be stimulated to attract more fortune into the life by selecting a jewel which correlates to the harmony mapped into the birth chart.

A birth-stone is a gem ruled by the Sun-sign. The Ancient Magi held that before choosing a gem which corresponds to the Sun-sign, the neophyte should first determine the harmony or discord of his natal Sun. If the Sun is afflicted, the gem will attract adversity unless the person uses directed thinking and induced emotion to overcome the condition.

In scanning birth-stone lists put out by various jewelers you may have noticed a vast difference. To satisfy my curiosity, I obtained a jeweler's list of birth stones. Here the list is given merely by months, not by dates corresponding to the signs of the zodiac.

January, garnet. February, amethyst. March, bloodstone or aquamarine. April, diamond. May, emerald. June, pearl or moonstone. July, ruby. August, sardonyx or peridot. September, sapphire. October, opal or tourmaline. November, topaz. December, turquoise or lapis lazuli.

Not being students of astrology or occultism, jewelers are ignorant of the law of correspondences. They push the sale of certain stones by assigning them to the zodiacal signs or months according to their fancy. Sometimes the amount of stock on hand determines the assignment as well as the fashion trends.

Compare the above list with the following correct talismanic gem for each zodiacal sign and planet given in the ancient Hermetic tradition.

Aries, amethyst. Taurus, agate. Gemini, beryl. Cancer, emerald. Leo, ruby. Virgo, jasper. Libra, diamond. Scorpio, topaz and opal. Sagittarius, red garnet and turquoise. Capricorn, onyx or chalcedony. Aquarius, blue sapphire and lapis Lazuli. Pisces, chrysolite, commonly called peridot.

The Sun, sunstone. The Moon, oriental moonstone. Mercury, meteorite. Venus, amber and coral. Mars, lodestone, hematite or bloodstone. Jupiter, Chinese jade. Saturn, jet.

The stones names in this list are those which for the most part lend themselves to fashion and the art of jewelry making. If it is unwise to obtain a certain gem (due to financial reasons or to the fact that no "live" specimen is available) it is quite as advantageous to use the gem for the sign in which the best planet is located in the birth chart.

Instead of guessing or assuming which planet or sign maps the most harmony in the horoscope, consulting a cosmodyne report for each individual birth chart. In Chapter 8 of *Astrology of Childbirth** you will find cosmodyne reports demonstrated.

In the legend and folk-lore which surrounds gems, various supernatural qualities have been ascribed to certain ones. Volumes could be written as regards this fascinating subject, but let it suffice to view a few of them.

The amethyst, symbol of sincerity, was an antidote for poison, dispelled sleep, sharpened the wits, promoted chastity, and according to Pliny was a sure cure for intoxication. The agate, emblem of health and wealth, sharpened the sight, averted storms and gave the wearer graciousness and eloquence. The Mohammadans held that it cured insanity if powdered and given with water or apple juice.

Beryl was the favorite stone of divination and when reinforced with potent incantations was supposed to tell the future and review the past. The emerald stopped hemorrhages, was cooling to fevers, and it was used to strengthen and preserve the eyes.

The ruby was used as an amulet against plague, poison, sadness, and sensuality. Jasper was good for lung trouble and would save the wearer from drowning. The qualities ascribed to the diamond include the power of curing insanity and epilepsy. When powdered, it was considered as an excellent dentifrice. But in the Middle Ages it was supposed to be a poison classed with arsenic.

A topaz was held to avert sudden death. The person who wore a turquoise needed no accident insurance, the stone having protective power. The red garnet was a protection against thunder before lightning was known to be an agent of destruction. Onyx and chalcedony were carved into beautiful cameos, which when worn would cure melancholy.

The sapphire was considered the symbol of constancy, truth and virtue, and if placed over the heart imparted strength and energy to the wearer. The influences of the peridot have never quite been captured by fable, because for generations there was no original source. Even the mineralogists were confused as to its classification.

The precious opal is literally covered with legend. It is the symbol of

*D.C. Doane. AFA. Tempe AZ. 1988

hope. But for years its reputation suffered from the superstition which claimed it to be unlucky. However, it regained its lost fame and popularity through Queen Victoria. Her Majesty demonstrated in many ways that she admired this fire-flaming stone.

When each of her daughters married, she gave them opals as wedding gifts. This act as well as others concerning opals received much publicity. Evidently she had a good motive, for her colonial subjects in Australia discovered opals at that time. Through successful propaganda, she showed her disdain for the superstition that opals were unlucky. Then, the opal was so royally reinstated that it held a high place in popular favor. Needless to say that the Australian exports increased handsomely.

The bloodstone was looked upon as the symbol of courage and wisdom. Because of its great magnetic attraction, it is the center much legendary interest. One tradition asserts that it originated at the crucifixion of Christ from drops of blood taken from His side by a Roman soldier. Even today, there is a bust of Jesus Christ done in bloodstone in the French Royal Collection in Paris. The work was planned and executed so that the red spots of the stone appear realistic in their resemblance to drops of blood.

Because of the mystical properties attributed to it, the ancient Egyptians and Babylonians used the bloodstone for seals and charms. They believed it to contain great curative powers.

According to the lore of lapidaries and many writers who have conducted considerable research, we find that many of the same qualities are tied in with several stones. Further, it is quite impossible to divide all of these stories which concern themselves with the occult properties into clear-cut channels referring to definite signs and planets. Why is this so?

In the light of our discussion at the beginning of this chapter, should we assume that unknown to the wearers, gems in one case were beneficial and yet in others detrimental to 'building in' charter vibrations of a spiritual nature? Could it be due to the ignorance of the law of vibration?

In choosing your jewel in the zodiac, select the one which will enable you to live a fuller, deeper, more constructive life. The key is in your birth chart.

Chapter 10

THE ACCIDENT SYNDROME

Think over the past year. Did you have a major accident? Or several minor accidents, such as cutting your finger, tripping up the steps, bumping into furniture, burning yourself, or bruising your fingers in a door jamb?

If you have had recurrent accidents, psychologists will file your case-history under accident prone, a term applied to people who have the accident habit.

Many research projects have been conducted with similar reports presented by each group of researchers. One survey revealed that of all accidents which occur, only 17 percent stem from mechanical defects. A Safety Council study which covered a period of five years indicated that seven-tenths of one percent of auto drivers were responsible for 27 percent of the traffic accidents.

In following the cases through to other departments in the subject's life, it was revealed that people who have accidents while driving or while on the job also have accidents in the home and during their recreation periods. The accident habit forms a consistent trend through most of their activities. The chronic ones have as many as twenty to fifty accidents in one year alone.

Rigid tests have been conducted by companies which employ drivers, notably cab companies and trucking concerns. Even though all mechanical defects were removed, working environment controlled and tests made on fair weather days, the accident rate will not change. So the managers selected the drivers with a high accident rate, took them out of the driver's seat and put them to work in the maintenance and other departments. These men were watched closely over a period of time. They still had accidents. They were accident prone.

Such tests as these began to pile up and psychologists were beginning to find certain personality traits appearing with regularity in each case studied.

Take the case of Miss A. an attractive girl of twenty years, she was popular and sincerely desired to get married. But in six months she had been given the brush-off from two attractive, eligible men.

Then one night she was given the third brush-off. When she was telling a friend about it, she started to light her cigarette, and the whole matchbook went up in flames, burning her hand quite severely. After dressing the burn, she decided to have a cup of coffee. In fact, she felt so much better after talking out her problem with her friend that she felt like having some breakfast. While frying the egg, the fat in the pan popped and bit of it flew to her face leaving a small burn on her cheek. Later she burned her tongue on the hot coffee.

You may think that is exaggerated. However, under the emotional strain a person's attention is directed away from the job at hand and onto the trouble. Suggestion offers a pattern to the subconscious mind. All sorts of inconvenient and sometimes tragic things can happen. The everything happens to me attitude is vitalized with so much thought energy that the person is fulfilling the law of attracting just such negative events into his life.

Personality traits which were commonly found in the accident group by the psychologists dove-tail with the astrological constants for accidents.*

Two-hundred timed birth charts of people who have all kinds of accidents including those involving violence of all sorts -- burns, cuts, wounds, drowning, broken bones and falls -- show a prominent Mars. Next in prominence are Uranus and Saturn. In the cases of poisonings of many kinds as well as in cases of asphyxiation, Neptune and Pluto were commonly prominent. If automobiles were involved in the accidents, Mercury appeared prominent in every instance.

*Astrology: 30 Years Research. D.C. Doane. AFA. Tempe AZ. 1956

Positive Benefits of Astrology

After a study of the case-histories and horoscopes, it is quite evident that people who have a prominent Mars, Uranus, or Saturn in their birth charts have decided predisposition toward accident. Any one of these planets would emphasize accident. But if two or all three of them appear powerful, the accident tendency is stressed.

The power within the individual which really attracts the accident is the psychokinetic activity of the thoughts within the subconscious mind. It is quite common for a person who has been the victim of an accident to say he had a strong hunch that something was going to happen to him. As has been pointed out many times, superstition is often synonymous with auto-suggestion.

The person who breaks a mirror and believes that bad luck will result quite often experiences some discomfort. He cannot blame the broken mirror. Because the negative thought he feeds to his subconscious mind works to bring about the mishap. The negative thought form suggested to the mind is revitalized by his sureness that some such incident will occur. He demonstrates the condition which he has built within himself.

This is a psychological process that is set in motion regardless of the motive behind it. In the case of placing faith in a rabbit's foot for luck, the forces set in motion are positive. We hold the thought that the rabbit's foot brings good luck. In reality, the four factors of demonstration have been fulfilled: Formulation, visualization, vitalization, and realization.

This psychological law plus the astrological findings should ease the way for correcting the accident habit, or at least minimizing it. First, the accident prone person should consult his birth chart, or a certified astrologer to discern where the major difficulty lies. Then he can utilize the power furnished by correct thought activity to attract harmony instead of discord. See Chapter 2 in the book *Astrology of Childbirth**.

Chief among the characteristics found common to this group was impulsiveness. Even though there is plenty of time, most of the people who have the accident habit are always in a hurry. They are tense, restless, and often make decisions without analyzing the conditions involved.

*D.C.Doane. AFA. Tempe AZ. 1990

Here we see the fiery aggressiveness usually associated with Mars. Correction will result by reconditioning the aggressive though-cells to attract events other than accident. Usually, a discordant Mars will map thoughts involving anger, hurry, combativeness, and irritation. Such thoughts should be channeled into constructive, deliberate, and planned endeavor.

The natural antidote for discordant aggressive urges is the group of thoughts called the domestic urge, ruled by the Moon. Therefore, the mental alchemist says the mental antidote for an afflicted Mars is the Moon and what it stands for.

During periods of stress the thoughts should be channeled into a soothing peaceful expression. Deliberate calmness in taking advantage of opportunities to help others will direct the discordant energy from self out toward others. If this is accomplished successfully, then there is not energy left to attract accident. Success may not come on the first try. But the accident prone person needs to persevere and repeat this approach many times.

A study of the case histories used in the research revealed that many of these people were quite fatalistic in their attitude toward the misfortune that came their way. Some thought they marked from birth with bad luck, others felt divine punishment was their due.

The truth of the matter is that they were victims of their own emotional conflicts, which built up to such huge proportions within their own minds that the psychological principle operated to attract accident.

As a man thinketh, so is he. The old axiom applies here, but what he should *think* to prevent accidents can only be found in the horoscope. Everyone is a distinct individual and has a horoscope that is different than anyone else's. As the planets break and form into newer patterns by progression and transit, a person responds to environment, both inner and outer, in a different manner.

Even if a person does not have many accidents (is not accident prone), there are times he will be more susceptible to them. Research shows these times coincide with progressions involving those accident planets: Mars, Uranus, and Saturn. Usually another zodiacal aspect will enter the picture and map in a clear manner where the conflicts lies.

The value of Astrology is not only to point out what type of thoughts,

Positive Benefits of Astrology

feelings, and actions will attract the best of all things to the native. Even the well-adjusted person needs to watch these times of possible accident which Astrology has uncovered. The progressed horoscope gives the periods to watch out for.

Chapter 11

THE YOUTHFUL OUTLOOK

When we first met the Barlows, they were a middle aged couple who had moved to the West Coast. They looked worried and tired; certainly older than they were. Their narrow viewpoints kept them isolated.

Several years had gone by before we heard from them again. The Barlows came to call one afternoon, and to say we were shocked and surprised is to put it mildly. Shocked and surprised not by their call on us, but by their appearance -- how vital and happy they were. They appeared years younger than the last time we had seen them. As we talked, they told a story familiar to most counselors.

Lacking advantages, they had started to stagnate back home. They were stuck in a rut, especially as regards to education. They never even thought of learning anything new (Hadn't they always gotten along okay?) Their recreation consisted solely of sitting in rocking chairs on their front porch, discontentedly watching the world pass by.

But the cosmopolitan vibration of coastal living perked up their ears, and they opened their eyes to the myriad adventures of Southern California life that abounded all about them. They took a giant leap forward by starting to fulfill all the laws of tapping the fountain of youth. Indeed, they are a happy *young* couple even today.

Moon and Mercury are surely the most important planets of youth, because certain types of thinking prolong the life and help to keep us young. If we stress harmonious thinking ruled by these planets -- the change and novelty of the Moon, and the intellectual activity and curiosity of Mercury -- we keep young.

Although the physical body deteriorates as we grow older, the brain functions, if we allow it to through instant use, until shortly before death in most cases. Many famous people of yesterday and today in the older group are excellent examples that the brain power need not wane with advanced age. True, in age some are no longer pliable of body, but they have brilliant intellects which cope with problems in all fields -- art, politics, economics, banking, agriculture, etc.

Among those who were still mentally active before passing were; in the field of physics Albert Einstein (1879-1955); in politics Herbert Hoover (1874-1964); in art Grandma Moses (1860-1961); in letters George Bernard Shaw (1856-1950); in the theater Estelle Winwood (1883-1984). Two living examples are George Burns born in 1896 and Helen Hayes born in 1900.

All of these people contributed to our way of life, each in his own field, yet all of them were considered aged from the standpoint of physical years, However, in their mental attitude, they would be considered young.

The brain will atrophy if it is not used. Thus insurance of keeping young is to look for new and ever newer interests as well as improved and progressive ways of doing things. If today's cook was placed in a kitchen of fifty years ago, he would rebel. Why? Because he and his kitchen have progressed with the times.

In addition to seeking a new interest, youth must be served with enthusiasm. If we build enthusiasm into our lives, we can face and solve daily problems much easier, as well as tackle the new interest we select in this adventure of living. Youth also *plays*. So we must balance our work-a-day world with some recreation. Each of us has his own idea of recreation. Therefore, each should select his own field in which to get relaxation. Another positive benefit of astrology is that we can interpret the fifth house in our horoscope to find out which recreation would be best to ease our tensions.

Venus also plays a role in the youthful attitude. The harmonious expression of thoughts, feelings and actions in our social and family life are important to a poised and integrated personality. Venus type thinking is a natural antidote for thoughts which pop up into the mind under Saturn discords, such as worry, fear, selfishness and discouragement. These type thoughts tend to attract old age.

Venus rules the emotional side of life, and when we lose all emotion, the vital life force is also lost. Ruling love, art, music and romance, Venus portrays the things which are conducive to youth. Take love, for instance. You have probably seen a middle-aged couple fall in love. If you have, you will have seen a transformation of those people -- they will appear ten years younger. Love is certainly an attribute of youth.

If a keen zest for living is maintained, monotony will be avoided. Proof of this statement in its relation to youth can be reached by watching a group of children at play. They are playing first one thing and then another. Nothing holds their attention for a long period of time. If they are forced to stay with one aspect of play for a long time, they become restless and rebel in no uncertain terms.

There is another important reason why we should avoid monotony. If we do the same thing all the time, we get into a rut. It is comparable to the nerve that is stimulated at short intervals of time over and over again. Soon the stimulation need not be added, as the reaction will take place in its absence. As there is no deviation, the habitual reaction becomes so dominant that flexibility and adaptability are prevented. Adaptability is a first requisite in overcoming difficulties, with which we are faced day in and day out. Some large, some small.

A youthful outlook is composed of interest and activity. A certain curiosity is present. Action is a must. When a person retires from his career or business, he should have a hobby into which he can throw all of his energies and interest. If he fails to, there is a loss of interest and action. That man becomes old. When the person retired, he planned to live and lounge for fifteen or twenty years, but his stay here on the physical plane is shortened because he allowed his brain to atrophy.

Sometimes we unwittingly place our values on the wrong things. This can happen in any department of life. As for growing old, often gray hair, wrinkles and the thickened waistline are taken as the signs of age. In reality, it is the *thinking* upon which we should evaluate age. It has often been said, "You are as young as you think and feel."

A helpful practice to adopt is take inventory of our own thoughts from time to time, to insure that the negative and unyouthful type of thoughts are banished before they have a chance to become a habitual reaction. Here is a list of traits all reflecting the unfavorable expression of the youth planets -- Moon, Venus and Mercury.

How do you rate as a youthful thinker? The more times you answer *no*, the more youthful you are.

1. Do you get more enjoyment out of discussing other people's lives than in striving to make your own life interesting?
2. Have you stopped making new friends and settled for the companionship of just one closely-knit group?
3. Are you afraid to do things on the spur-of-the-moment invitation?
4. Do you keep rehashing in your mind the small annoyances and unpleasant incidents of life, instead of taking them as a grain of sand?
5. Do you live through the lives of your children; that is, do you get a great satisfaction out of their accomplishments instead of your own contributions to society?
6. Do you take a negative view of life -- always expecting the worst to happen?
7. Have you failed to try some new gadget which came on the market in the past few years?
8. Did you fail to investigate some new line of learning; reading up on it and applying the principles to the practical plan of living.

It will be the exceptional and unusual person who can answer *no* to these questions. However, your score will give you an inkling as to whether your mental attitude is youthful. This holds whether you are sixteen or sixty, because youth is a state of mind in the last analysis.

When a person advances in age and refuses to feel sorry for himself, refuses to make his children feel responsible for him, and goes about his business making his life intensely interesting, that person is happy. He is

48

youthful. He is respected and admired and has a real place in his community. He expresses the youthful outlook.

Chapter 12

DIFFERENCES MARKED IN PERSONALITY

When Alice T. was a child, her life ran smoothly. Her parents were the understanding type who always encouraged her to make her own decisions. She had many advantages, she was exposed to refinements and culture early in life. At fourteen years of age she was faced with a difficult situation, one which affected her reputation with the other children in school.

Because her experiences up to this time had not been painful, she met the situation squarely. She did not feel fear. Instead of trying to get around it by means of lies, she was truthful regarding the circumstances which brought the situation about.

Upon seeing this frank and truthful attitude, her parents were pleased. So instead of punishing her for "running with that gang" as the gossips put it, they praised her for the square and forthright manner in which she acted. This was the beginning of the honesty habit-system for Alice. She grew into adulthood to be a well integrated person, because her early environment stamped her desires with the good and cultured and the true.

Then there was Charles E., who more or less grew up by himself. His folks didn't bother much about him. They saw that he had adequate clothing and enough food, but at that their interest seemed to end. For the rest of the time, Charles was on his own.

Because he did not get the satisfaction of being someone in his own home -- the feeling of significance -- he attempted to get it from the boys in the street. He tried to be a big-shot. To accomplish this goal, he started to steal. First, it was just an apple from the fruit stand. He would brag to the other kids how he got away with it. Later, when that story was old and no one listened to him any longer, he moved a little further uptown, where he shoplifted a cowboy holster. He wasn't caught. Of course, his folks had no idea what was going on.

His confidence at this point was overbearing. He had developed a swagger. He found that he could get away with filching objects, so the habit-system of stealing was firmly embedded in his subconscious mind.

When Charles grew into manhood, his parents were able to procure him a good position with a bank through business acquaintances. Later when he was placed in a position of great trust, he was unable to resist the powerful temptation to become an embezzler. Charles is serving time at a penitentiary. His cunning acts all through life were the result of undiscovered lies and the absence of discipline. Both he and his parents contributed to the eventual outcome.

Beryl C. was a stunning child. Her mother had ambitions of her becoming a motion picture star. But that never did seem to work out. However, the feeling the mother had was transferred to the child, who became self-opinionated and insisted upon being the center of attention. When she could not have her way, she resorted to crying fits, sulking and throwing tantrums. Finally, to shut her up, her mother would give in to her whims.

The child learned a lesson. The next time she wanted anything, she would throw another tantrum, probably much worse than the last. These actions through early youth built up a behavior pattern which was liberally sprinkled with outbursts of violent temper and uncontrollable behavior.

She grew into womanhood and took with her the youthful habits of the past. She is temperamental and hysterical. Her doctor's bills are stupendous. She has visited a string of specialists, trying without success to find the cure of "her nerves".

Naturally Beryl's disposition is not conducive to a happy marriage, because she is self-centered and has never gotten along with another person in her life. So she has had four husbands. Again, we find that early environment had a great deal of influence on her future behavior patterns.

We naturally adopt certain habit-systems for sleeping, for eating, for recreation, for social life, for study, and many others. If we but watch, we can see the same development in others. But it is impossible to judge another person by viewing only one habit-system, and expecting that one alone to reveal his total personality.

That type of judging character is no more valid than a cartoon of

Mikhail Gorbachev picturing mostly the birthmark on his scalp, or a caricature of Bob Hope in the form of a ski-sloped nose. No, one aspect is not enough to give the total picture. Some of the most notorious criminals of the past have revealed the Jekyll-Hyde aspect. They were exceptionally loving parents and faithful spouses. In their domestic area, they were conditioned socially, but in certain other areas, they were decidedly anti-social.

Therefore, if you happen by for a visit as the family sat down to dinner of an evening and saw Public Enemy #1 cutting up his little son's meat with care, and when helping the little woman clear the table afterwards, you could not assume from these actions alone that he was a respected member of the community. This, in spite of the fact that respected members of the community are assumed to be as solicitous of wife and child.

The fundamental urges which underlie all human life must be satisfied, if the personality is to be well adjusted. All normal persons have these basic desires -- the desire for security, self-respect, the respect of others, sexual expression, etc. In fact, all basic desires may be divided into the groups symbolized by the ten planets in the zodiacal chain. The manner in which these desires find expression is through experience.

If the experiences of each type are associated with the desires mapped by a planet, you can see that no two people are alike. This is true because no two people have the same birth chart. The formation of the four basic astrological factors -- planets, signs, aspects and houses -- is never the same in any two charts. His basic character plus the conditioning he receives from experiences and environment along the pathway of life make him what he is at any point in life.

In the cases of the three children above, the planetary patterns stand out. Alice had been given the conditioning energy and environment to transmute her horoscope trends.

But Charles had to grapple with the desires that come under a discordant Saturn in unfavorable aspect with the Sun while Beryl's trouble was indicated by the Sun opposition Mars.

Here, briefly, are the types of desires associated with the ten planets. If you have one planet strong in your horoscope, this prominence (power) indicates that the corresponding desires are outstanding in the makeup of your character.

SUN: Desire is for significance. Build a habit-system of gaining significance by contributing something of benefit to society. Then self-approval from a job well done gives constructive satisfaction to these desires.

MOON: Domestic desires, the wish for a home and children. Here the best satisfaction for desires will be found in taking pleasure in caring for the family or those less fortunate than self.

MERCURY: Desire for intellectual activity. Develop the habit-system of getting a kick out of over-coming obstacles. Concentrate on and analyze the factors involved to find the best solution.

VENUS: Desire is for affection, beauty and companionship. Get pleasure out of social contacts, wisely directed affection and wholesome entertainment.

MARS: Desire is for aggressive action. Direct the aggression toward building up rather than tearing down. Some energy may be used to fight or to repair a sick body. Engage in athletics or dancing.

JUPITER: Desire is for cheerfulness and abundance. Develop the habit-system of faith and good will to all, curbing the appetites to void extravagance.

SATURN: Desire is for safety. In seeking security, develop the habit-system of planning your activities, having faith, and shouldering the necessary responsibility. Key is long range planning.

URANUS: Desire is for originality.

NEPTUNE: Desire is for the ideal and perfection.

PLUTO: Desire is for cooperation.

Chapter 13

DO SUN-SATURN AFFLICTIONS DENY SUCCESS?

In our thoughtless moments, we quite naturally blame the planets for the harmony or discord which enters our lives. Of course, this attitude is erroneous from the standpoint of dynamics in the art and science of astrology. In the final analysis, all of the planets are harmonious and travel about the heavens in their orbs according to law and order.

Intermediate step-downs of power are the factors we often over-look. Astral energies radiated from the planets impinge upon the subconscious mind. Then, and then only is there a discordant or harmonious reaction. The centers of energy and the manner in which they are formed into complexes in the subconscious mind is portrayed by the birth chart.

If Joe's chart shows "good" aspects, then when the Mars center is stimulated, harmony will be attracted because of the conditioning for these energies to act precisely in such a manner. But if John's Mars "center" is stimulated, he will unconsciously act discordantly because his Mars is, as we say, afflicted.

Yet, through a knowledge of astrology, John can recondition the thoughts which compromise that Mars center and build up a habit system of reacting harmoniously. We cannot blame the planets. Let's face it! The dial to harmony or discord in life is within us. All we need to do is apply the key -- the horoscope -- to know how to recondition and adjust conflicting elements in our basis make-up.

One of the aspects viewed with much alarm is the affliction --

conjunction, square, sesquisquare or opposition -- involving the Sun and Saturn. If there was a bogey-man in the stellar closet, which there most assuredly is not, this aspect would fit him. Many a fine person has succumbed under such stimulation. On the other hand, it has acted as the trigger to great achievements.

Specific cases point to General Dwight D Eisenhower, who under progressed Sun in obstacle (square) aspect conducted the great invasion of World War II. Former President Woodrow Wilson ascended to office under Sun opposition Saturn. With it came the responsibility of organizing the country for war and establishing peace for the Allies. John L Lewis, under progressed Sun conjunct Saturn, organized labor unions, a task which demanded the planning of Saturn and the authority and leadership of the Sun.

A prominent Sun in the horoscope indicates that the conditioning of the native has been along lines which involve significance. The corresponding mental center is composed of power thoughts. Experience which stimulates the drive for significance has been uppermost. The psychological drive may express on a high level through seeking self-respect in society, or on the lower level through selfish dominating authority.

Saturn corresponds to the safety thoughts, which have been organized by vivid responses along the lines of self-preservation. If through the process of conditioning the safety thought-cells or the sun thought-cells have been marked with painful associations, the birth chart reveals a discordant aspect between the two planets.

Simplified, the combination represents a conflict between two mental factors. Painful experiences associated with the complex bring events which are discordant into the life. In particular, the mental energies are conditioned to attract loss and hardship, limitations and responsibility with the people, objects and things mapped by the houses representing the specific departments of life affected.

In astrology, regardless of what factor is under consideration, there is always a two-fold pathway for energy expression. One expresses through destructive activity, and the other through constructive activity. As stated before, the dial is within us. All energy is neutral until it is picked up and transmitted by the subconscious mind. The key is found in diverting the energy into a constructive channel in spite of the aspect which may appear in the chart.

Desires of the thought-center mapped by Saturn will always strive for safety, attract work and responsibility and the natural constructive trend if given encouragement of the right kind. Constructive Saturn energies manifest as system, order, economy, and careful planning. likewise, the desires of the thought-center mapped by the Sun have a constructive trend by seeking significance and authority which will contribute to the happiness and success of both the individual and society.

More than a theory, these psychological factors have been exemplified many times over in the lives of prominent people who have had great success in all fields of endeavor. It was demonstrated in the 1940's when World War II was raging. A short food ration program was dubbed *Hooverising* because he had organized soup kitchens during the depression. His birth chart reveals a Sun opposition Saturn. Because of his reputation as an organizer and ability for detail, he was appointed Food Administrator, and later Relief Administrator after the war.

Both posts brought him in direct contact with Saturn type conditions - -distress, want, poverty. Further, it was during his administration as President that the great depression occurred. He lost much of his popularity at the time. But his inherent abilities mapped by the Sun-Saturn opposition worked constructively in the re-organization plans for the Government.

Both Notradamus, the famous prophet, and William Lilly, early astrologer, had the Sun opposing Saturn in their natal charts. Many writers, among them Havelock Ellis, and painters, Rembrandt for one, had that opposition aspect in their horoscopes. All of the people mentioned in this chapter gave a constructive expression to the Sun-Saturn thought complexes.

They took pleasure in contributing something to benefit society. Their contributions were better than others in the field. Therefore, they satisfied the drive for significance (Sun) by benefiting others and taking a great deal of joy in the doing, rather than expressing the energy in destructive channels to gain authority through force and slavery, using the attitude of rule or ruin.

A constrictive Saturn manifestation is outstanding in the lives of these successful people. It coincides with doing the job after careful, insightful forethought and planning, which involved deep thinking, attention of detail and, above all, persistent plodding. They developed courage to shoulder responsibilities, having a strong faith at the times when it appeared that the bottom was ready to fall out.

Experience and observation teaches that harboring fearful and selfish thoughts proves to be most unprofitable. Inevitably such negative thoughts are accompanied with loss, poverty and diseases of the chronic type. Saturn thoughts are sluggish and demand the social urges symbolized by Venus which maps the natural antidote to find adjustment. Pleasure -- natural or acquired by inducement is of prime importance in transmuting energies mapped by an afflicted Saturn.

A prerequisite to success is will-power, the important factor in character building. The energies corresponding to the Sun are noteworthy of consideration, because they compromise the deep-seated and permanent part of the subconscious makeup. They indicate the traits of character which are strongest and which have the most resistance to change.

Ancient alchemists placed gold under the Sun's rule. Gold is the finest of all metals. They held that if these Sun traits were refined by directing the energies to universal welfare, rather than to self-aggrandizement, the finer constitution of man, his mental make-up, would quite naturally refine, purify, and spiritualize all other thoughts. A lazy person would never achieve success under the Sun-Saturn complex, because Saturn thoughts attract work and responsibility. Usually that involves long and hard effort to attain accomplishment. People who permit these desires to remain in the state of organization in which they occurred at birth, merely pacifying them and *doing what comes naturally*, are drifting with the tide.

Furthermore, when these people allow environment, either physical or subconscious (aspects), to stimulate these existing complexes at different times into greater activity, without doing something to correct the flow of energy, are wasting God's gift to man. That is the ability to achieve self-mastery through induced emotion and directed thinking along the lines which will contribute most to the self and to society as a whole

The true alchemist, by use of the astrological key, works continually to overcome the defects in his character. He knows that he alone is responsible for his character today and for what kind of a person he will be in the future. He also knows that Sun-Saturn afflictions do not deny success. Conversely, he grasps the opportunity present to build character and become a better credit to his community.

Chapter 14

HANDLING MARS SQUARE NEPTUNE

There was a typical pea-soup fog, and rain had practically inundated the Evacuation Hospital in Korea. There was the negative, complaining vibration which more often than not surrounds such places. Discouragement and hopelessness marked the patients. Over-worked attendants were snappy and irritable.

The nurses had to walk about in hip-boots, plowing through sloshy mud up to their knees. Most of them had kidney trouble. There as very little time for leisure. In the few odd moments, they sat around a pot-bellied stove, easing their tired bodies to capture what little heat there was. The place was cold and gloomy.

Everyone knew everyone else's business. The atmosphere crackled from such confinement. Alice sat there bitterly eyeing her companions. Her thoughts were dour. Here, I have been a registered nurse with plenty of experience, and these young squirts walk off with all the promotions. She thought back to the time the Aries nurse tried to boss her around. She mused, " *Well! I fixed her, even if I did sound off.*"

As long as I can talk faster than the rest of them, they cannot put anything over on little Alice. As the many antagonistic incidents passed the screen of her mind, she recalled this was the time to take action. Talking wouldn't solve the problem.

Quietly she eased away from the group and stole into the place where medical supplies were stored. The unlocked cabinet was her target. She reached in, removed a bottle, locked the door, and just quietly went to her bunk.

As the shifts were changing next day, Alice did not report for duty. Upon investigation she was found in a dead stupor. The empty pill bottle on the floor beside her told the story. She had attempted suicide. After sleeping two days she awoke. She was extremely weak, but otherwise none the worse for the action.

Her Mars had progressed to the square of birth chart Neptune. Her environment was conducive to the negative expression of this aspect. Upon checking her case history, it was found that she imagined many of the situations that tormented her mind due to the Neptunian influence. When she was released from duty, her record stated: Psychoneurosis; reactive depression, situational with suicidal tendency; unstable disposition.

After a short period of hospitalization, she was checked out. For the next three years one tragedy after another dogged her footsteps. The Mars-Neptune square had come to full bloom. Alice finally had the good fortune to contact astrology, which held an answer for her. But it took a tremendous amount of work for her to redirect her thought patterns.

She learned to erect her chart and calculate the major and minor progressions herself. That was in the days before the computers. Then with the aid of *Mental Alchemy**, she overcame recurrent depressions and desires to end it all.

Her story had a happy ending, which is unusual, because most individuals will not exert themselves to the extent necessary to alter firmly established conditions in the mental set-up. By faithfully applying the mental antidotes and closely guarding her thoughts, she corrected the condition which lead to procuring an excellent nursing position, teaching occupational therapy on the side. The Mars-Neptune energy was then directed in a proper manner.

The process through which we learned is called conditioning. At all times there is some degree of pleasure or pain, harmony or discord, accompanying this process. These feelings of pleasure or pain as regards

*C.C. Zain. The Church of Light Inc. Los Angeles CA. 1936

various past experiences form the *conditioning* energy. Planets represent a definite thought-family in the subconscious mind. If two planets are involved in a discordant aspect -- semisquare, square, sesquisquare or opposition, the quality of the conditioning energy is painful.

These zodiacal aspects symbolize specific trends and focal direction of the desires represented by the planets. Desire, which is energy straining to be released in some activity expressed in a manner which is painful or discordant in relation to the department of life (horoscope house) in which the planet falls or rules, if nothing is done to change the situation.

It is the discordant relationship of thoughts (planets), conditioned by pain, that is responsible for disease and misfortune. Therefore, a study of the afflicted planets gives the astrologer a key to the trouble. It indicates the specific habits of thinking which need to be altered to change the unfortunate condition in life. Alice's trouble came from discordant aggressive urges (Mars) in obstable (square) aspect to the utopian urges (Neptune).

By major progression, Mars travels approximately forty-six minutes a year. However, other times Mars moves slowly and thus stays within orb of an aspect for a period of years. When in progressed aspect, the orb of influence is one degree applying and one degree separating the perfect aspect. Therefore, when Mars is moving about forty-six minutes a year, the progressed aspect it forms remains within orb for about three years. Progressed Neptune moves hardly at all, just a minute or two a year.

Due to this slow Neptune motion, the Mars-Neptune setup is in a potential state for about five years. A long time aspect such as this one grows on a person. He feels *natural* under the influence. However, symptoms of depression should be watched, for the negative trend is a deep under current. A small amount of accessory energy, such as a slow moving transiting planet, could upset the apple-cart.

To handle the Mars-Neptune energy intelligently, we must first determine just what happens in the subconscious mind when Mars forms the square aspect to Neptune. Each planet represents definite thoughts, closely tied in with feelings of discord or restriction. Therefore, each one coincides with definite trends in the behavioral pattern.

Positive Benefits of Astrology

Aspects of Mars stimulate thoughts which have to do with strife, haste and a tremendous increase in the out-go-of energy. In the subconscious mind, thoughts are aroused which influence the behavior through destruction (or construction), initiative, sex, aggression, fighting, eating and drinking. Furthermore, objects and certain types of people in the environment which are ruled by Mars become important in the life. Such as soldiers, surgeons, mechanics, cooks, war, machinery, steel, intoxicating drink, etc.

Huge amounts of Mars energy seem necessary for worthwhile accomplishments, as witness the horoscopes of the great persons in history who have added to the welfare of society. But accomplishment results only from successfully directed energy. An afflicted Mars calls for Moon thoughts as an antidote. Application is through metal alchemy. A determined effort is called for to alter the habitual thoughts.

Moon-thoughts may be expressed by supplying help to the helpless, making home life more pleasant for the family, and doing that *little extra bit* to make those about you happy. When feelings of strife, anger and antagonism enter the consciousness, make a deliberate effort to replace them with Moon-thoughts. Take action by doing social work, or engage in a hobby that will help others. Induce the emotion of pleasure, *feel* great joy in what you are doing. In this manner you build a constructive channel through which the energy can flow and satisfy the Mars desires in the subconscious mind.

At the other end of the square is Neptune, a higher octave planet. These energies endow the nervous system an unusual sensitiveness to other vibrations. As Neptune is the octave expression of Venus, representing the social urges, people figure strongly in the thoughts. The magnified sensitiveness tends toward illusory impressions, exaggerated expectations (followed by disappointment), and fantasy thinking. The imagination is increased under Neptune aspects. Thoughts are aroused which express in daydreaming, wishful fantasies and promotional schemes.

Objects and people indicated by Neptune are the important environmental factors, such as gas, movies, extra-sensory-perception, drugs, promoters, mystics, oil, aviation, etc.

Neptune maps an energy which is essential to round out a healthy and productive personality. If it were not for its dramatic trend, many of our everyday occurrences would become most boring. But the quality of Neptune can lift a situation from drudgery to pleasure. When Neptune is afflicted, correction comes through applying Saturn thoughts to give stabilization. Also needed are Sun-thoughts to give a more positive attitude toward self-respect and significance.

Saturn thinking brings the problem out of the realm of fantasy into the practical life of past experiences. Then, exaggerated ideas of Neptune are examined carefully in a methodical manner and faced for just what they are. The addition of Sun-thinking gives vital, courageous thoughts and displaces negativism. Then significance is realized on the plan of reality, rather than in wish fulfillment of the imagination. In this manner, it is possible to avoid discordant thinking of Neptune, which coincides with repression, poisoning, disease, infection, as well as disappointments over fallen idols, etc.

Discordant aspects represent trends of thought which in some manner block the highest type of living. The repression and conflict they picture is often unknown to us until revealed by a study of the birth chart. Once we recognize these trends, we can release energy through proper channels. Energy is neither discordant nor harmonious until captured and released by the subconscious mind which stamps the trend upon that energy.

Persistent directed thinking applied with pleasurable association will eventually train the subconscious to release the energy in a harmonious manner. True, under most afflictions much more application is necessary. But the duality of nature is seen even in the expression of energies mapped by each planet. This expression has a higher and a lower manifestation. We cannot change Mars energy into Venus energy. But we can most certainly direct the Mars energy into a constructive expression.

Alice demonstrated the fact by harmonizing the energy of a Mars-Neptune square and directing it into construction action, both at work and at play. She has found that we must face life, for we cannot run away. Wherever we go, we take ourselves along. Bluffing and putting on a front are not necessary, for if we are big enough to admit our inadequacies, other sincere people will believe in us.

Alice gained control over her inner desires and thoughts in relation to external environment, realizing through her studies the important factors that bear on her own social life. She gained confidence and understands how to use the energies of a Mars square Neptune.

Chapter 15

AT WHAT DEGREE IS YOUR TEMPER

From the moment of birth, each of us has to make adjustments to the constantly changing circumstances both in the physical environment and in the environment in which our subconscious mind functions. The pattern is never the same. But due to our basic natures, as portrayed by the natal horoscope, certain trends and reactions are more or less predictable if nothing is done to change the character.

We carry about with ourselves little bundles of habits. When they contact environment (outer or inner) of like vibration they waken into vibrant aliveness, but they may lie dormant at other times in the absence of this stimulus. Some people form habits of impulsive emotional release instead of controlled emotional direction. When they meet an obstacle or when they are opposed or blocked from doing something, they become enraged.

That reaction expresses on the animal level where there is little power of intelligence. The behavioral response usually coincides with the lower expression of the aggressive urges, mapped by Mars. When stimulation brings about this condition, there are ways to avoid its negative expression. According to natural law, this energy *must* express along Mars channels. However, we can apply intelligence to make the best of becoming emotional. In order to accomplish the transmutation successfully, a little knowledge of the law is necessary.

We are living and functioning in the physical world. Thus we have a physical body. Because our life and activities are focalized on two planes of expression, we also have an astral body. The difference between these two realms of life is one of velocity.

Modern physics assumes that anything moving with the speed of light looses all physical properties and no longer exists on the physical plane. That there is an inner-world where velocities are greater than those of light has been proven conclusively by psychical researchers and astrologers. This psychic phenomena and the action mapped by astrological energies demands just such high velocities in the inner-world in order to manifest.

The inner-world is called astral, which means stellar or pertaining to the stars. It is through this body that planetary energies affect us. We may question the extremes of these two planes. One has such low velocity! The other such high velocity! We know a current demands a medium through which to function. Likewise, our two bodies require a medium through which to contact each other. The physical velocities are too low to directly affect the astral and vice versa.

Electromagnetic energies are approximately at the velocity of light, forming the boundary-line between the two planes. (see Diagram A in Physical-Astral Transmission*). This electromagnetic belt is the medium which makes possible the contact between the two planes. The electromagnetic energies. often called the etheric body, are associated with both physical and astral substance.

Planets radiate astral streams of energy which bombard the astral body, and by means of electromagnetic energies, there is a pronounced influence upon our thoughts, our behavior and events which come into our lives. The astral radiation of each planet has a basic key tone, and through the law of resonance imparts energy to the groups of thought-cells (basic urges) in the subconscious mind having a similar key tone. Thus it may be said that the radiations act as a trigger force.

If we stimulate the aggressive urges, an impression is imparted to astral substance, which is set into motion and effects the astral plane where the subconscious mind lives. It is through our thoughts that we build on either the astral or the physical plane. The increase of a certain vibration will effect the

*Astrology of Childbirth, D.C. Doane AFA Tempe.AZ 1988

mind and the emotions. However, the mere adding of power is merely one factor in personal adjustment.

Adding more aggressive energies could end in one or two results. Either it will bring the temper up to a hot *blow-off,* or it can, under intelligent direction and controlled association, set forces into action which will result in constructive, aggressive endeavor of a successful nature. In both instances there is a release of energies, both Mars in nature. One is destructive. The other, constructive.

Mars is considered the minor malefic in the chain of planets. It corresponds to various qualities in our makeup! Energy, courage, forcefulness, violence, resistance, and aggressiveness. Its great resistance and forcefulness mark the energy as a tool forcefulness mark the energy as a tool of construction or destruction. It is an accepted fact that sufficient energy of this type is necessary for any worth while progress and accomplishment.

Without the energy Mars gives, drive and confidence would be lacking. Fear and anxiety would make inroads into the consciousness. All activity is always in the direction of the greasiest desires. So we never should try to kill out any desire. Rather, this very energy should be channeled and given direction for the welfare of the mind and body.

Another characteristic of the aggressive type is zeal and enthusiasm. No great work is accomplished without it. The urge also gives the fight and struggle to resist unwanted influences. Therefore, if a temper is controlled, we have a huge volume of constructive energy at hand, which can be turned into a valuable asset. Then there is no exception of defeat. Any obstacle which gets us down, no longer absorbs the best of our energy. Rather, we use that same energy in a quick snap back to try a new approach. Much the same type of fight can be brought to bear upon unwanted and poisonous thoughts.

Other than these general qualities pictured in the birth chart, Mars appears in different patterns in each individual horoscope. One person may have Mars as the strongest planet, receiving strong harmonious aspects from Uranus and Mercury. This configuration commonly maps unusual mechanical ability. His fellow worker may also have strong Mars and in aspect to Uranus and Mercury, but the aspects are discordant.

Positive Benefits of Astrology

That co-worker may have the mechanical skill, but with it will follow physical accidents at work unless he redirects the energy. Obstacles will be placed in his pathway to success along mechanical lines. Another man may have a very weak Mars and no mechanical ability at all. These examples are cited to point up the individual differences which occur. At birth, people are not equal in ability. As they tread the path of life, their opportunities are not the same. In nature's school each of us is undergoing different training. Aspects of Mars picture the degree in which the aggressive urges have been conditioned painfully or pleasurably.

One of the most destructive activities which coincides with an afflicted Mars is temper, or *getting mad.* Although we often place the blame for it upon someone else or some object, others cannot upset us emotionally unless we allow it. Blame rests upon our own emotional reactions. The way we think is of the great importance.

If we give an unfortunate situation much though, the astral form is built and vitalized to the point where disastrous consequences may result. A huge volume of energy will be called forth. Excessive and uncontrollable emotion is not likely to occur if we keep focusing the attention of our minds upon what there is to do about correcting the situation.

Emotional stimulation is good for the mind and body only when it expresses it purposeful thinking and behavior. It gives us the ability to go at a situation aggressively when we are called upon to meet it. If, however, no control is attempted, the most common result is mental confusion.

That explains the negative side. but the positive action of energy expressing under Mars aspects gives a wide field for self-development. It is through experiences of the Mars type that we can learn tolerance. The forcefulness and enthusiasm we hold is of no value until we develop the ability to recognize that others have a different viewpoint and their conception of things is the result of their own experiences and observations.

If we build a wide tolerance and realize that others are entitled to their own opinion and ideas we can learn to argue without becoming angry. Through this approach, we are able to recondition any negative emotional reaction which is present.

Harshness and anger act as a boomerang. When others try to injure us, it is through ignorance. On treating us so, they are only injuring themselves. No one can hurt our feelings unless we allow them to. When the other fellow shouts and criticizes us in a moment of anger, and we shout back, thus building up anger, we only hurt ourselves.

If we attempt to replace vengeful thoughts, clear thinking and action will enable us to meet the situation more constructively. In this attitude, there is not implication of a *door-mat*, but of taking a firm stand. When the emotions are under control, the opposition can be overcome without harm to the other person, with a view to improving the situation. Violence will be avoided as well as the degree of your temper.

Chapter 16

ARE YOU FAMILIAR WITH PLUTO?

A knowledge of astrology opens the doorway to many secret vaults and sheds light into corners which once appeared darkened by shadows. It is the key to a richer, fuller life, both here and hereafter. In approaching new fields of endeavor or unknown subjects, this knowledge comes to the aid of the student.

Life reveals itself as a fascinating venture having a basic purpose of the progression of the soul. One such venture is along the bypaths of ancient mythology, where if we but utilize astrological symbolism the esoteric significance of these often-told fables is revealed.

Turning to Greek Mythology, we find that Saturn was king of the universe, and had three sons: Jupiter, Neptune, and Pluto. When he was dethroned these three quarreled over the division of the universe. As a result of the conflict Jupiter fell heir to heaven and earth, Neptune took the sea, and Pluto became king of the stygian realms, the region of death and funerals.

Even though considerable research has been undertaken as regards the planet Pluto since its discovery in 1930, there is still a wide field for investigation. Pluto rules the watery sign of Scorpio, and it is the higher octave of the Moon. The natures of revengeful Scorpio and the tenacious Moon lend an insight into his expression. The word *tenacious* is used here in the sense of the emotion expressed by a mother cat when her kittens are attacked.

Pluto has a dual expression, each side being quite distinct from the other, for he is an extremist. The manifestation is in relation to groups, the best through co-operation and the worst through coercion.

The lower-Pluto influence closely corresponds to the sign Scorpio, which is pictured in the sky by a scorpion to symbolize the base qualities of selfishness, revenge, cruelty, and treacherousness. However, the eagle which soars to spiritual heights portrays the best quality, and Pluto expresses thus on its higher side.

Upper-Pluto influence may attract opportunities to join groups in doing some truly spiritual work, afford avenues for inner-plan activity and extrasensory perception (ESP), and/or work to break up crystallized materialism in elevating the political, economical and social conditions of society. This pioneering inner-plane work and social welfare has been associated by many astrologers with the spiritual side of the sign Aries. These hold that Aries is ruled by Pluto.

The Lower-Pluto influence, however, is the side the planet has the most shown in the period after its discovery. This is an emotional quality which cause other astrologers to hold that Pluto rules Scorpio, that its exaltation sign is Leo, and that its harmony sign is Aries. Timeliness requires that we associate Pluto with Scorpio, at least until such time as its better side will be exerted toward Earth, when man has learned to transmute his emotions spiritually.

Because of its pronounced duality of expression, the motivating principle involved is two-fold. That is, the trend of thoughts, feelings and actions under Pluto stimulus may be toward highest human attainments or to underworld gangsters, crime, and subversive activities.

In its expression as the higher octave of the Moon, there is a negative sensitiveness present which permits the tuning-in upon thoughts of others on both inner and outer planes of life. The Moon expresses the mother principle in the family unit, and Pluto expands this principle to embrace the whole of society as a universal family unit.

Just as the extreme inclination of Pluto's orbit defies the conventional standards of zodiacal limitations of other planets, so does it represent digging deep into dark pools of iniquity or soaring to the white light of spiritual horizons.

"The descent of Avernus is easy; the gate of Pluto

stands open night and day; but to retrace one's steps and
return to the upper air -- that is the toil, that is the
difficulty."   Virgil.

Avernus was a lake situated at the entrance of the infernal regions, which was
so poisonous that birds, in attempting to fly over it, fell lifeless into its waters.

As king of the underworld, Pluto had rule over death, just as the sign
Scorpio rules the eighth house of the natural horoscope. As ruler he was a
dictator, and therefore we would expect to see this influence manifest in
modern history. The analogy is seen in the parade of events which had
occurred after the discovery of this planet.

Dictators of many types have filled the headlines: Hitler, Mussolini,
Joseph Stalin, Franco, Ayatollah Khomeini, Saddan Hussein, Fidel Castro,
Mu'Ammar Al Qadhafi, to name a few.

When Pluto entered the sign of Leo (whose worst quality is
dictativeness) in 1939, the Pluto groups in various countries started an all-out
struggle for world supremacy, thus World War II. In mythology much the
same dictatorial and subversive activity is told.

One of the gods, Pitithous by name, wished to marry a goddess
residing in the underworld. In spite of the grave danger to be faced, he
descended to the lower regions to bring his love back to light. But Pluto seized
him and chained him on an enchanted rock at the gate of his palace. Pitithous
was left to his fate.

A renowned physician, the Greek hero Aesculapius, who was endowed
with great healing powers, at one time succeeded in restoring the dead to life.
As this threatened his kingdom, Pluto ordered the bold physician be struck by
lightning, and he was killed. Pluto wields a drastic and forceful weapon when
engaged in destructive activities.

Perhaps one of Pluto's first steps after he became king of the
underworld was to kidnap Persephone, the goddess of vegetation, while she
was gathering flowers in a field. He took her away to his dark realms, and she
became his queen. Then the countryside was stripped of vegetation. Ceres, the
goddess of agriculture, was her mother. When Pluto stole her beautiful and
beloved daughter, she lighted her torch and in a chariot drawn by winged

snakes searched all the lands.

Finally Pluto agreed to allow his queen to stay with her mother part of the time each year. So Persephone helped her mother superintend the growing harvests during the summer. Then the autumn, like the seed, she returned to the lower regions (earth) with her mate, only to come forth again in the spring. The fable demonstrates what two-fold expression of Pluto.

In Mundane Astrology, the cycle charts (as well as in charts of nations and cities) show a prominent Pluto at the time of kidnapping. It was shortly after the discovery of Pluto that Congress enacted the Lindbergh Kidnap Law.

In reviewing some of the major kidnappings since then, we found Pluto prominent in each instance. At the time Congress passed the law, Pluto was in opposition aspect to aggressive Mars in the Pluto Cycle Chart (February 20, 1864).

In 1933 Pluto opposed Venus in the sky. At this time five kidnap cases occupied federal agents. Charles Boettcher in Denver (February 12); Mary McElroy in Kansas City (May 27); William A. Hamm, Jr., a banker in St. Paul (June 15); August Luer in Alten, Illinois (July 10); and Charles F. Urschel in Oklahoma City (July 22).

Except in the first case, all kidnappers were apprehended and sentenced to life imprisonment. One woman was involved. On November 6 of this same year Brook Hart of San Jose, California was killed. His two accused kidnappers were lynched by a mob (Pluto).

Pluto turned retrograde in 1934 and formed another opposition to Venus. Three major cases was reported. Edward G. Bremer of St. Paul (January 17); William F. Gettle of Los Angeles (May 16); and Mrs. Alice Speed Stoll of Louisville (October 10), The kidnappers were apprehended and sentenced.

In 1935 Pluto turned direct in motion and again touched off the opposition to Venus. Only one major kidnapping case was reported. George Weyehaeuser of Tacoma (May 14), whose kidnappers were convicted and imprisoned.

Pluto trined Jupiter in Scorpio in 1936. Charles Mattson, 10, was found dead in Tacoma. His kidnapper escaped.

Jupiter opposed Jupiter in the sky, and in its Cycle Chart Pluto bowed into Leo, then retrograded back into cancer. 1937 revealed two kidnappings: Charles S. Ross of Chicago was found dead (September 25); and Arthur Fried of White Plains, New York (December 4), whose body was alleged to have been burned in a public hall in Manhattan Borough. Kidnapers were convicted and executed.

Mars conjoined Pluto in 1938. At the same time in its Cycle Chart Pluto formed the inconjunct aspect with the Sun (rules Leo). Pluto was located in Leo, ruler of the natural fifth house (children). Two cases involving children were outstanding: Peter Levine, 12 of New Rochelle, New York (February 24), whose body was recovered, but the kidnapper escaped; and James Bailey Cash, Jr., 5 of Princeton, Florida (May 28), whose kidnapper was executed.

In 1940 Mars formed a fixed square aspect with Pluto in Leo (children). Marc de Tristan, 3, of Hillsborough, California was recovered alive and well. His kidnapper was apprehended and sentenced to life imprisonment.

When Pluto opposed Mercury in 1942, it also entered into a trine aspect with Neptune (hospitals). It was this year that Ruby Evelyn Cremeans walked into the Saint Ann's Hospital and pointed a revolver at the attendants in order to kidnap an 18-month old baby. FBI agents followed her through several cities, finally apprehending her with the baby. She was sentenced to serve twenty years imprisonment.

It is significant to note that with the entrance of Pluto into the sign of Leo all of the major kidnapping cases on official record involved children, which are represented by the fifth house of the birth chart, over which Leo has rulership.

The most drastic example of Pluto activity was the case of Suzanne Degnan (January 6, 1946) of Chicago. William Hierens, 17, student of the university, strangled and dismembered this 6 year old girl. He was charged with some hundred other crimes of a Pluto nature. Pluto was square Pluto at the time in its Cycle Chart.

Other events of a sex-crime nature followed as the year wore out. The 1946 sky revealed the violent aspects of Saturn conjunction Pluto, both squaring Mars in Scorpio. Not a peaceful combination.

Chapter 17

MAKE THE MOST OF YOUR DAYS

It is true that there is a propitious time for every enterprise, and those versed in astrology are competent to chose the time. As a result of a vast amount of research conducted by astrological groups, in America as well as aboard, the natal chart with the major and minor progressions and transits is now considered the most effective index to starting a project of any kind. With the information thus gained, electional and horary charts in conjunction with mundane cycle charts are then consulted.

In this manner the astrologer is able to select a day on which the planet(s) corresponding to the nature of the project is well aspected and at the same time does not stimulate discord in the basic birth chart. Furthermore, these mundane cycle charts offer a picture of general national trends, and the electional and horary charts give a map of the life of the venture. With these road maps at hand, the person is enabled to avoid many hindrances and obstacles to the success of his plan. He can take advantage of the favorable indications by applying the philosophy of astrology.

Another less scientific method of choosing fortunate times is to look for a day in the ephermeris when the Moon is in favorable aspect to the planet ruling the nature of the venture. This is the approach used to select the best times during the year to undertake any one of hundreds of events in *Lynn Palmer's Astrological Almanac**. With this handy manual to consult, you

* AFA. Tempe AZ. Annual.

won't have to look these favorable times up in the ephermeris. To carry the method further, after the day is selected, we can also decide on an advantageous planetary hour during the selected day in which to start the project.

Ordinary activities do not need such painstaking details. Many of them we are compelled to take on regardless of the aspects forming in the sky or in the astrological charts. All things being equal, the particular focalizing of specific planetary vibrations dominates each day of the week. The energies within the person corresponding to that planet are stimulated in a broad manner. The planetary rulers and the names of week-days present a descriptive picture of the various natures.

These names are all of northern origin and tie in with the seven basic planets. Sunday is from the Anglo-Saxon Sunnaen Daeg, Sun day, which is ruled by the vital Sun. One of the first religious groups on earth were the Sun worshippers of the heliolithic culture. Ever since that time, the trend has been to worship on Sunday. This is in order when the nature and functions of the Sun are accounted for. All energies upon earth are radiated from the powerful Sun. Without it, life would cease.

Therefore, the subconscious thoughts on Sunday prompt us to attend church in order to receive spiritual upliftment. Sun stimulation also influences the vitality, thoughts of pride and self-esteem. As it rules the sign of Leo and the fifth house of a natural horoscope, children and entertainment are prominent in the Sunday picture. Hardly a home today does not have the casually tossed funny-papers strewn on the living room floor. Sunday is a day of rest, a day for renewing vitality; a day for capturing and storing energy to be released the rest of the week. It provides balance to our work-a-day routine.

Monday is for the Anglo-Saxon Monaen daeg, the Moon day, and the second day of the week is ruled by the domestic Moon, which is closely associated with the home, the common people and everyday life in general. It governs the watery sign of Cancer. Since time on end Monday has been associated in the mass consciousness of generations with wash-day. These domestic energies can be used advantageously in catering to the needs of the whole family.

Monday is the day to deal with offspring, the sick and helpless, tasks involving liquids, women, nurses, and people in general. The Moon rules the subconscious mind and is impressionable. Its watery nature strongly influences the emotions. There is a tendency to become over-sensitive, to harbor hurt feelings about inconsequentials, and to lean toward gossip. If these thoughts, feelings, and actions begin to manifest, turn the attention to some constructive activity, replacing the Monday blues with aggressive endeavor.

Tuesday is from Tyr, the Norse god of war and athletic sports, hence Tyr's day. Tyr was also known as the god of battle, or the sword god. The third day of the week ruled by the energetic Mars. It is intimately associated with doctors, surgeons, mechanics, sports, and aggressive activity. Therefore, Tuesday is a day of great energy. Plan to use it to your best advantage. In the old nursery rhyme, it is a day dedicated to ironing. With all of our modern equipment and modern *cloth*, hardly is a whole day needed for this domestic chore. Still, the day will hold much energy for you.

If the expenditure of this Mars flow is not watched there is a tendency to do things hastily, or to over-act or drink. If the thoughts, feelings, and actions become over-stimulated in this direction, it is a good plan to pause, and relax completely, to balance the vital energies of the mind and body. When you resume the day's chore in a calm manner, all sorts of Mars mishaps can be avoided: Burns, cuts, combativeness, sharp talk, anger, etc. Probably one of the best antidotes for over-aggressive feelings is to sit comfortably, and while rocking hum the tune *Rock-a-bye Baby.* You will involve the smoothing influence of the domestic principle, the mental antidote for an afflicted Mars.

Wednesday is from the Scandinavian Odin, the early German Woden, hence Woden's day. Odin is pictured sitting on his throne overlooking all heaven and earth. There is a raven upon each of his shoulders (symbolizing the duality of Gemini), who fly over the world each day and upon returning report all about what they have seen and heard. The fourth day of the week is ruled by the intellectual Mercury. This is a day for mental interests, expression, and thought activity. The sign of Gemini and the third house of a natural horoscope are associated with Mercury. Therefore, it is a day for study, writing, speaking, traveling and all mental activities.

This is a good day to answer those letters you have set aside for *sometime when I have a minute.* Wednesday also holds a warning. Under Mercury stimulus there is a tendency to scatter the energies. Do not plan too many chores. It is better to plan too few and do a thorough job of them. Remember that too much mental activity burns energy to the point of depletion. A good balance is a brisk walk in the fresh air, stepping in rhythm and breathing deeply. The system is revitalized, for the lung's come under the rulership of Gemini.

Thursday is from Thor, the strongest of the gods and men in Norse Mythology, hence, Thor's day. Thor has three sacred possessions; a hammer, a belt of strength, and a pair of iron gloves, symbolizing a protective influence. The fifth day of the week is ruled by benefic Jupiter. Perhaps the most outstanding influence stimulated by this planet as regards everyday life is its relation to business, selling, rather than buying which is governed by Saturn. But the greater benefic, as Jupiter is called is closely associated with publishing, finances, banking, charities, good-will, religion, and good luck in general.

Under its rays, which coincide with hope, optimism, and abundance, there is a warning. Increased optimism and excessiveness may result. If the thoughts, feelings, and actions are over stimulated by these energies, a good antidote is to apply the reasoning faculties to find out just where you stand. Through such analysis and discrimination, Thursday's chores will be accomplished in a constructive manner. The faith of Jupiter will see you through.

Friday is from the old German Frigu, or Frey, the Norse god who presided over rain, sunshine, and the fruits of the earth, and his sister Freya, the goddess of music and flowers, hence Frey's day. The sixrh day of the week is ruled by the gracious Venus. The astral energies of Venus affect social affairs, the emotions and the artistic tastes. Under her warm rays, we are influeneced by thoughts and feelings of friendship, affection, laughter, and beauty. As Venus rules flowers in general, this is a good day to assemble floral arrangments, which will give you and your family pleasure throughout the weekend.

Venus rules sweets. So why not take advantage of this time to prepare your special baked delicacies as a surprise for the family. Or, purchase a box of sweets for a friend or companion. Fashion also comes under this influence.

Take the opportunity to replenish the wardrobe or jewlry on a Friday. Good Venus hobbies are dancing, singing, dramatics, the crafts, etc.

Venus, like all other planets can symbolize a negative aspect, which is usually summed up as *the way of least resistance.* The trend will be counteracted with a little beforehand planning. Then your day will be constructive, productive, and pleasant if your attitude has the wholesomeness and beauty of Venus.

Saturday is from Saster Daeg, which in turn is from the Roman Saturnus, hence Saturn's day. The seventh day of the week is ruled by stabilizing Saturn. Saturn's vibrations are associated with work and responsibility. Economy and loss also present influences. Thus we sometimes frown upon Saturn's presence. But a truly balanced oneness is composed of vibrations on a higher level of all the planets. Saturn is no exception.

He has his duties in furnishing the constructive energies to our lives. In fact, he is symbolic of thoughts of safety, system, organization, and persistence, all of which are necessary in accomplishing any worthwhile endeavor. On the the other hand, if we become negative, and allow the negative energies to master our thoughts, feelings, and actions, worry, selfhishness, greed, and fear result.

Saturday is the day many house clean. The correct approach to this necessary but often gruding chore is expressed by the higher side of Saturn. Organize your equipment, arrange your thoughts into a smile to appreciate accomplishment, and go to it. Take joy in the excellent job you are doing. In this manner negative Saturn will not have a chance to rear his head, and your job will be complete in record time, leaving you with an exalted feeling. Pat yourself on the back for a job well done.

Make your week full of happy days.

Chapter 18

THE MOTHERHOOD PRINCIPLE

"The Moon, that pale, silvery, glowing light that illumines the darkness after the Sun has sunk in the west, has a very marked influence upon everything on this earth. Like a queen she rides forth into the inky blackness of night, enveloping the whole earth with a glow of wondrous beauty. Like an empress she stalks forth at dusk, showering her benefits upon us all. Clothed in soft, silvery light like pale hammered precious metal, she reminds us of all that is gentle and beautiful, and awakens the poetical nature in us all. The Moon has the beauty of a woman, while the Sun has the strength and dominance of a man. Like king and queen they each hold alternate say over the great blue dome of the sky"

S. Gargilis

When a period is selected for a holiday or to venerate a special occasion, we can trace a correct astrological correspondence. Sunday is sacred to the Sun, or ego of the human being. Monday is sacred to the Moon or washday. Tuesday is dedicated to ironing and is ruled by the fiery Mars. Mercury rules Wednesday, the day of baking, and the wheat grain from which flour is made.

At Christmas when the Savior is born, the Sun starts to travel through the zodiac from south to north declination. At Easter when all the christian peoples look to the east and sing, "He is Risen!"; surely He is. The Sun reaches its exaltation in Aries, where its creative energies are greatest. On Thanksgiving, a day of prayer and thankfulness, the Sun has entered Sagittarius, the natural ruler of the ninth house of religion and philosophy. On Labor Day, the Sun is located in Virgo, ruler of the sixth house of the natural chart (work), where labor is performed.

On Mother's Day, the second Sunday in May, the Moon is posited in its exaltation sign of Taurus, the Sign of its highest expression. At this time, the Sun appears in the third decanate of Taurus, which is pictured by the constellation Auriga, showing a charioteer who is in control of the solar (Sun) forces. A mother goat (Moon), clutching two kids, has jumped into his arms for protection. While there is anticipation of the harvest to come after the spring planting, so also is the Sun and Moon a representation of the fruitfulness of the female sex of mother. The decan keyword is *mastership*. In addition to birth, Mother's Day indicates that a true master controls the forces of nature and employs them to benefit others, just as the mother cares for and protects her offspring.

During this period of the year people since ancient times always venerated the mother principle. The Moon in Taurus better pictures motherhood. Even more so than when it is located in the zodiacal sign of Cancer, because the Taurus motivation stabilizes the mother principle. Perserverence coupled with the domestic urge is best adapted to raising children.

Because woman bears the chief burden of replenishing the earth, it is fitting to venerate motherhood. However, extremes are not in accord with universal law. Some take glory in being virgins, overlooking the fact that the only way the Creator has of replenishing the earth is through motherhood. Self-exaltation over non-fertility is a false satisfaction for the ego. May is the time for planting of the seeds, and the Divine Plan would be interfered with if the planting did not take place.

As the Great Plan of Life unfolds before us, we cannot see that any mistakes were made, regardless of surface appearances. Certainly, we can give way to childish temper if we feel that the earth has gone to ruin. On the other hand we have the option to consider calmly the fact that perhaps the Creator has some ideas that we do not know too much about. The Plan has proceeded up to now, even though we have witnessed periods in the past when it appeared as if there would be very little light tomorrow or the next day. We had come to a dead-end street. Periods such as these occur along the road of life.

Because we are here today shows that we overcame the obstacles presented. What seemed to us a loss of everything does not hold. What we assumed to be totally unsurmountable objects were not so at all. Our being here today proves that all the stress and strain, the uncertainty of the essence of light were just groundless fears in our own minds. If we had spent just a little of that energy on the subject of Life, analyzing our plight, we would probably see that there was a basic experience to justify our turmoil. Even today, in the presence of unsettled conditions, we must stick our chin out and say, "This thing IS going to work out!" Then we can help avoid emotional upsets.

When world and personal affairs are chaotic, it is time to practice faith, patience, and perserverence, the mother's attitude toward her child. We must determine to make the best of our lives with the tools we have, for obviously we have a mission in the great scheme of things. Individual creativeness can be used to advance personal well-being. Potentials for creativeness, whether developed or not, are buried deep.

Within each of us exists not only the exact counterparts of all the universe but the power to put these potentials through the creative mind so they will develop, just as the child does within the womb of the mother. These spiritual children already exist as potentials for all of us. The birth chart is the key to finding them. Solution comes through the interpretation of the twelve signs, the twelve houses, the ten planets, and the ten aspects.

Unfertilized seed is like undeveloped potential. We must start to build the temple (Solomon's) in our own soul. By using our creative power we initiate the progress of our divine plan. In order to fertilize the potentials to growth, we must employ the mother principle, which is the stable emotion and perserverence that permits us to carry on day after day, week after week, year after year, trying to be our very best selves. No one can take any part from us that is our heritage, nor can anyone add to our characters. Therefore, we must build the proper desires and channel controlled emotions toward a shining goal.

One of the greatest blessings is the perfect organization of the Divine Plan. As none can take away from nor give to our characters but ourselves, it rests with each of us to whether or not we will be fertile creatures, having a perpetual Mother's Day. The choice depends entirely upon our mental processes. The motherhood principle within is ourself. It is either the "rough ashlar" or the unnoticed diamond in the rough. When the diamond has been ground and polished (spiritual qualities cultivated), it becomes the priceless jewel of the soul.

If the diamond is to be polished, it must be done by our own hand. The Father-Mother God gave into our keeping not only all potential to become a spiritual being, but He also gave us the power to direct our own destiny. We are free to harvest as much as we will, or let our fields lay fallow, permitting the diamond to become lost in the mud.

Regardless if we are male or female, we can all be nurturing mothers to the potentials with us. We can nurse the faulty children through their periods of spiritual sickness, feed the week ones, and assist in building character. Then we can look with pride and say, "That is my child!"

The *mastership* of the Mother's Day decanate of Taurus implies the controlling of the forces of nature, according to natural law, and using them to cooperate with, and benefit others.

83

Chapter 19

DEMONSTRATING YOUR HEART'S DESIRE

Demonstration should not be a strange word to anyone these days. All types of schools -- religious, metaphysical, and astrological -- teach the art of demonstration. Students of these schools have reported some outstanding and successful results. If you have never demonstrated anything, then you are failing to use your inherent mental power to insure your own happiness and progress.

There is a fine line between just what one should try to attract and what would be unwise to attract. The best measure of the worth of a particular demonstration is to decide if it is going to hurt anyone else. Or, will it deprive another person of something?

In times of crisis, such as earthquakes, floods, hurricanes, etc. when homes are razed, many people are forced to double up with in-laws and maybe even strangers and live in small, crowded accommodations. At these times many more people need housing than there were houses to take care of them. Viewing one of these catastrophic periods opened my eyes to one facet of demonstration which before had not seemed so important to me. I had been so busy with my duties for a number of years that I had not thought of demonstrating anything out of the line of those duties.

Joe and Mary Herrod were the ones who opened by eyes. They had been occult students for many years. When they learned they were going to have a baby, they knew the road ahead would be different and maybe not so easy. You see, they lived with her folks and her brother and his wife lived there

84

also. As it was only a small house, they were really cramped for room already. When they told me the news, I said "Well, why don't you put your minds to work and demonstrate a house? You can do it, if you work together."

To my surprise, they turned thumbs down on the idea. Buf their reason for doing so has give me many moments of thought and mediation.

Mary explained that they would not want to try to demonstrate a house, because it might take one away from someone who needed it more than they did. When the resistance of environment is so great, it is well to analyze all factors before making a decision to attract your heart's desire.

I admire her unselfish viewpoint, but I must admit that at first I could not fully understand her reasoning. The more I thought about it, the clearer the point became that it is a serious and grave responsibility to make a decision to demonstrate something. It is a thing which will in most cases affect others than oneself.

If you pursue this subject very long in your meditations, you will open many doors for thought. It was a fruitful subject for me, and it brought to mind many facets of the situation. When a person takes something from society, that is, when he obtains wealth in one of its many forms -- money, a house, a car, etc., he should be ready to pay his debt to society by returning wealth in some form.

We can't really kid ourselves into thinking that what we take from society is not the result of another person's efforts. When we face this squarely, we cannot but admit that we are indigent citizens if we do not give an equal amount of equivalent wealth in return. Those people who take without a thought of giving in return live in spiritual poverty.

The man who has a wealthy spiritual estate is the man who contributes to the community for what he gets by using his mental powers to invent something which will greatly add to living conditions: to discover better methods of production and distribution; to discover better ways of organization and efficiency: and to strive for measures which benefit society as a whole.

After deciding if it is moral in a universal sense to demonstrate your desire -- that is, making sure that you are not hurting anyone through demonstration -- then it is well to consult your horoscope. Look to the influences in the house of the chart which reveals the affairs that are tied in with the demonstration.

For instance, if we want to demonstrate a house, we look to the fourth house of the horoscope. We study the sign on the house cusp, the planets located in the house or intercepted if any, and to the aspects of those planet(s) ruling the cusp sign. Now, we synthesize these factors. As a rule, we will find which avenues will aid us in attracting our desire.

Of course, we take for granted that you know all about the price you must pay for the demonstrated desire. In God's Great Plan, there are no free rides. Because of the Law of Conservation, there is always an exchange. In demonstration, one needs more than faith, he needs to pay in works. The old Bible saying sums the idea: "*Faith without works is dead!*"

Demonstration and its technique can be broken down into four steps: formulation, vitalization, and realization.

Step I: Formulation. After carefully analyzing the possible effect upon others and deciding the thing is worth demonstrating, we must formulate a definite and clear conception of what we desire. This important for it is the basis upon which the other three steps rest. If the formulation is not definite and vacillates from one thing to another, then the results will likely be muddy and indefinite. This is so, because the *energies invoked try to fill out the image before the attention.*

Thoughts are powerful things; they make up the mental attractive force with which we work. Therefore, directed thinking is necessary to hold the image before the attention of the mind. after formulation, realization of a demonstration depends upon two things. One, the amount of energy you put into the mind-picture you have formulated; and two, the resistance offered by the physical environment.

Step II Visualization. To find out just what thoughts and things will help in the visualization of the subject can be determined by consulting the birth chart and the progressed positions of the planets. Certain groups of thoughts all work efficiently to help along the demonstration, while others will oppose it. The horoscope reveals the key to the opposition and will also show just what should be done about it to improve the. attractive force.

In visualizing the desire, see it in your mind as completed here and now. If you are demonstrating a house, see the whole conception of a house, not the parts, You limit the possibilities by viewing the parts in detail. If you start dreaming about that cute little broom closet, or that spacious rumpus room, you will be scattering your energies and whole deal might just fizzle out.

Step III : Vitalization. Here we work to develop effective mental energy. At first, you might think this can be acquired by using the objective mind alone, by directing it with force upon the sought after desire. That is only a small part of the procedure. Because of the mental properties of the subconscious mind, it is more effective to let the subconscious mind gain as complete an image as possible. Then the energy will be diverted into building up the thought-form, which comes about before the physical manifestation is seen. To accomplish this, suggestion and affirmation are employed in the usual manner. No thoughts of doubt or fear of wind blowing on the house built of cards -- one little gust will destroy the whole works. One negative thought can do as much damage.

Just wishing for a thing does not vitalize the desire. Rather than sit about listlessly waiting, take steps in the direction of the objective. If it is health to be demonstrated, read, and study about hygiene and diet, etc. This gives the subconscious something to work with. Or if you are writing a book, do the research in the field of your subject matter and let the subconscious go to work on it. Or it may be an invention you wish to demonstrate. Then you will need to read and study all material available on that particular subject. In demonstrating, we must assist the mental processes as much as possible. Undoubtedly it is possible to rid your garden of aphids (Plant disease) by using your mental powers. But how much more time you will have for constructive work if you take a trip to the corner and buy chemical preparation to do the work in a short time. In demonstration, we need to use a lot of common sense.

Step IV Realization. If you have followed and fulfilled the laws of nature, your desire is fulfilled. You receive just what you asked for and everything that goes with it. Perhaps you did not realize that the other things came with it as a matter of course, but there they are. Again you realize that it is important to carefully analyze a desire before setting out to demonstrate it.